Development and International Relations

Anna K. Dickson

Polity Press

First published in 1997 by Polity Press in association with Blackwell Publishers Ltd.

2 4 6 8 10 9 7 5 3 1

Editorial office:
Polity Press
65 Bridge Street
Cambridge CB2 1UR, UK

Marketing and production:
Blackwell Publishers Ltd
108 Cowley Road
Oxford OX4 1JF, UK

Published in the USA by
Blackwell Publishers Inc.
Commerce Place
350 Main Street
Malden, MA 02148, USA

ISBN 0-7456-1494-9
ISBN 0-7456-1495-7 (pbk)

A CIP catalogue record for this book is available from the British Library and has been applied for from the Library of Congress.

Typeset in 10½ on 12½ pt Palatino
by Ace Filmsetting Ltd, Frome, Somerset
Printed in Great Britain by Hartnolls Ltd, plc, Bodmin, Cornwall

This book is printed on acid-free paper.

Development and
International Relations

To my parents and David

Contents

Preface

The compelling impetus for this book arose from my desire to include questions of development in the teaching of international relations. This forms part of an on-going attempt to introduce students of the international system to the whole, rather than just the most powerful part, of that system. I found there were few texts which covered the Third World, its problems and aspirations, as an integral part of international relations. Caroline Thomas's *In Search of Security* (1987) stands out, and a second edition has been commissioned. I have subsequently unearthed new material, from disparate sources, and in the process met a number of people working in similar areas. Indeed at the 1995 British International Studies Association Conference the sub-group on Development and International Relations was launched, linking people from both disciplines.

Development and International Relations is both a critique of the exclusion of development from the discipline of international relations, and an attempt to rethink what development in the 1990s might mean in the context of a changing global order. In the process it examines the relationship between the global and the local and assumptions about universal progress, and highlights the increasing differentiation between and within states. In writing a book of such potentially wide scope I have been forced to make choices about what to include and what to leave out. I cannot claim to have covered all the relevant issues. I have chosen to concentrate on issues which both are relevant to the 1990s and beyond, and highlight the diversity of the Third World.

The writing of this book has proved both arduous and enjoyable. It would not have been possible without the help and support of a number of people. The Department of Politics at Durham has supported me throughout; indeed the bulk of the book was written while on research leave from my normal teaching duties. Encouragement to keep going has been provided in particular by Steve Welch, Jean Richardson, Soran Reader and Elvira Belaunde. Outside of Durham I am grateful to Caroline Thomas for feedback at the beginning of the project. Rebecca Harkin at Polity Press has never, it seems, doubted my ability to produce a good book and has always seen the positive side of feedback from anonymous referees. I am, of course, indebted to those referees for all their comments, which have helped to guide the book through its various stages. Last, but by no means least, my husband David has provided continuous emotional support and useful academic criticism, and typed my bibliography. Without all of this the book would not have been completed. It nevertheless remains my project and I am wholly responsible for the analysis and interpretation it contains.

Acknowledgements

The author and publishers wish to thank the following for permission to use copyright material:

Oxford University Press, Inc. for tables 4.1, 7.1, 7.2, 7.3 from *World Development Report*, 1994 by The World Bank. Copyright © 1994 by The World Bank. And for table 7.4 from *World Development Report*, 1986 by The World Bank. Copyright © 1986 by The World Bank. For material from the Commission on Global Governance, 1995, *Our Global Neighbourhood*. Also material in table 6.2 from Dreze and Sen (eds) *Hunger and Public Action*, 1989.

Cornell University Press for table 4.2 reprinted from Stephan Haggard: Pathways from the Periphery: *The Politics of Growth in the Newly Industrializing Countries*. Copyright © 1990 by Cornell University.

Diana Tussie for table 7.5 *The Developing Countries in World Trade* published by Lynne Rienner Publishers in 1993.

Every effort has been made to trace the copyright holders but if any have been inadvertently overlooked, the publishers will be pleased to make the necessary arrangement at the first opportunity.

List of Abbreviations

ACP	African, Caribbean and Pacific (states)
ACS	Association of Caribbean States
ASEAN	Association of South East Asian Nations
BNA	Basic needs approach
BOP	Balance of payments
CAP	Common Agricultural Policy
Comecon	Council for Mutual Economic Assistance
DFI	Direct foreign investment
ECLA	Economic Commission for Latin America
EU	European Union
FAO	Food and Agriculture Organization
FTA	Free trade agreement
G77	Group of 77
GATT	General Agreement on Tariffs and Trade
GNP	Gross national product
GSP	Generalized System of Preferences
HDI	Human Development Index
ICA	International commodity agreement
ICCH	International Commodities Clearing House
ILO	International Labour Organization
IMF	International Monetary Fund
IPC	Integrated Programme for Commodities
IPE	International political economy
IR	International relations
ISI	Import substitution industrialization
ITO	International trade organization
LDC	Less developed country
LPE	Liberal Political economy
MDC	More developed country
MFA	Multifibre Agreement
MFN	Most Favoured Nation

MTN	Multilateral trade negotiation
NAFTA	North American Free Trade Agreement/Area
NAM	Non-Aligned Movement
NGO	Non-governmental organization
NIC	Newly industrialized country
NIE	Newly industrialized economy
NIEO	New international economic order
NTB	Non-tariff barrier
OPEC	Organization of Petroleum Exporting Countries
PED	Political economy of development
PQLI	Physical Quality of Life Index
RIPE	*Review of International Political Economy*
SAP	Structural adjustment policy
TNC	Transnational corporation
UNCED	United Nations Conference on the Environment and Development
UNCTAD	United Nations Conference on Trade and Development
UNDP	United Nations Development Programme
UNEP	United Nations Environmental Programme
UNESCO	United Nations Educational, Scientific and Cultural Organization
WCED	World Commission on the Environment and Development
WHO	World Health Organization
WTO	World Trade Organization

Introduction

Development is both a concept and an activity. The trend towards globalization and greater integration of the world means that development can no longer be seen as an isolated practice. The prevalence of appalling poverty despite many years of development dialogue suggests that the concept, as it has been defined, is in need of rethinking. The phrase 'the question of development', used throughout this book, refers to the open-ended nature of this debate.

The empirical focus of this book is on the linkages between the Third World and the international system in the 1990s. Arguably the end of the Cold War has affected approaches to the study of development and international relations (IR); in particular, state-directed and non-market approaches have been dismissed. 'Openness', 'liberalism', 'market orientation' and 'competitiveness' (on a global level) are the buzz words for the Third World and the newly 'liberated' and post-communist societies. Does this scenario offer a brighter future for most of humanity? Have all other possibilities been obliterated by the logic of global change? These are important questions for any rethinking of the question of development.

The title *Development and International Relations* implies consideration of development questions in the discourse of the international system, which is IR. That is the discipline to which I am, broadly speaking, attached. The title does not assume that development is smaller than, and can be contained within, IR. Rather, questions of development are potentially much larger than any single social science discourse, because development is multifaceted and because, in its broadest sense, it is an issue which all societies face.

Yet to what extent is it meaningful to talk in terms of global development? Does it imply the sum of all developments, or is there something more? Can global development be a goal or an end in itself? What is at stake here are assumptions about universal progress, the nature of the relationship between the local and the global, and questions of homogeneity and differentiation. Development is not simply a technical solution; its history, both theoretical and practical, reveals the contested nature of these issues.

For example, European development theory viewed all states as treading a common path to the stage of high mass consumption. If global development meant anything, it meant industrialization (modernization) for all. Blockages to this end were to be found not in the global structures but in the domestic (internal) affairs of a given state. The dependency perspective, on the other hand, stressed the external constraints, linking underdevelopment in the periphery with development in the centre. The world was viewed as a single capitalist economy, the periphery a category of states almost doomed to perpetual poverty. Development has never been as simple as either of these perspectives, and they are not entirely mutually exclusive. A combination of internal and external factors is necessarily at work. Importantly, the context of development theory and practice is constantly changing; solutions applicable in one decade may not be applicable in the next. Thus the expansion of the global market place has tremendous implications for development. As Leys (1996) rightly points out, it is in the nature of an unregulated competitive system that some parts of the world will benefit, and others, unless they acquire the capacity to compete in the market, will not. They may nevertheless choose to chart 'another' type of development (see chapter 1).

The chapters in this book explore policy areas and issues which I consider to be important because they rethink traditional relationships between the North and the South and explode the myth of homogeneity in the Third World. The study is thus multifocal. It is concerned with several different dimensions of development. On the one hand it is based on the assumption that development should be seen not as something unique to poor states, but as part of the processes of change and transformation facing all societies. On the other hand it is clear that the development debate (surveyed in part I) has leaned too heavily on European ideas about economic progress and that development has been equated with economic growth and industrialization. Thus a recurring theme in the book is that although the question of development is universal, its interpretation will need to be contextualized in different societies. The issues covered here have been chosen to illustrate this.

The newly industrialized economies (NIEs) of East Asia demonstrate the success of economic growth through industrialization to an unprecedented degree. However, the ability of the environment to sustain such industrial growth throughout the world is questionable. The tension between preserving the environment and getting on with development can only be resolved if a new concept of development is embraced: sustainable development?

An often forgotten dimension of development is the social one, and here difficult questions about what makes life worth living reinforce the particularity of development. At the same time, the fact that many people cannot meet even their basic calorific requirements throws into question the global market as an efficient allocator of resources.

Trade has always been seen as crucial to the development process, trade being the engine of growth. Yet many societies have not benefited from the trade regimes they have been involved in. Nevertheless it is important not to fall into the trap of making assumptions about the perpetual poverty of Third World commodity producers. Some states (the NIEs) threaten the position of older industrial ones. The Uruguay Round of the General Agreement on Tariffs and Trade (GATT) demonstrated quite clearly that increasing diversity meant there was no single Third World interest.

The end of the Cold War has had significant implications for the question of development, for example through increased donor conditionality. Yet it also opens the door for a reconsideration of many of the issues which remain important to the development debate: security, the environment, peace, population and so on, all of which are interlinked. At another level there are no general solutions and no grand theories, simply individual case studies and comparative analyses of different states, regions and peoples.

As well having this empirical focus the underlying approach is one which attempts to steer between what O. O'Neill (1993) refers to as an idealized (or universal) and a relativized (or particular) account of what development means. The former approach argues that we are all moral equals, regardless of the accident of nationality. Consequently the presence of widespread and unnecessary poverty is a problem which should concern us all. This in turn has implications for the theory and practice of IR, the discipline of the international system. In particular, the prominence given to the principle of state sovereignty creates problems for dealing with, for example, the global distribution of resources, or the use and misuse of the biosphere.

The latter approach argues that development is not about a single universal ideal; rather it is particular to different social arrangements. Change and transformation have to be related to the particular values and aspirations of the social grouping under investigation. The development debate has relied heavily on European ideas about progress.

The approach taken here is that there are some universal parameters, such as meeting basic needs, but there are nevertheless different weights and mechanisms for the evaluation and interpretation of such needs. While development is concerned with the problems of all human societies, its interpretation must be contextualized.

Part I, 'Development Revisited', explores the theory and practice of development and argues for the question of development to be seen as an on-going discourse. Chapter 1 asks what the question of development in IR might mean. Chapter 2 questions the current terminology of development and the categories used to group different countries together. Chapter 3 surveys, as simply as possible, the main theories which have dealt with the question of development to date. Chapters 4–7 come under the heading of part II, 'The Global Economy and Development'. They variously survey the issues of industrialization, the environment, poverty, population and hunger, and trade. They challenge homogeneity in the Third World and are designed to show that different states face different domestic issues, and have responded differently to global ones. Part III focuses on 'The Third World in the Emerging World Order'. Chapter 8 looks at post-Cold War adjustments and the implications these have for development. Chapter 9 returns to the question of development, and what it might mean in this new global context. Importantly, the book tries to point towards a way to make the development debate meaningful.

Part I
Development Revisited

1 | Development and International Relations:
Theory and History

Introduction

This chapter examines the uneasy relationship between the question of development and the discipline of IR. While this uneasiness may in fact be the logical outcome of the manner in which both the development discourse and IR are constructed, it is not inevitable. This chapter begins by looking at the theory and practice of IR, and how the question of development has been excluded from the discipline. The chapter then explores what the question of development might contribute to the debate. The next section examines what a focus on the question of development in IR might mean. Does it imply that development theory is contributing its concepts and techniques to IR, or that IR is providing the case materials for the study of development? I suggest that IR should by definition include the question of development in a global context within its ambit. This demands at the very least a more inclusive and globally focused discipline.

The theory and practice of IR

'The systematic study of the relations between states had begun to take shape by the middle of the seventeenth century' (Olson and Groom, 1991, p. 1). Olson and Groom point to the emergence of the European state system with the Peace of Westphalia has been constructed by the West, typically in the UK after World War I and in the USA after World War II. Consequently IR has reflected the concerns of academics (and of policy makers) from these countries, and has not always been keen to engage in theoretical debates originating outside them.

The first of the so-called 'great' debates in IR occurred between two rival interpretations and understandings of the international system: the *idealist* (or Utopian) and the *realist* perspectives. While idealism perhaps had the potential to create a more inclusive discipline, realism, reflecting very much the post-war hegemony of the USA, narrowed the scope of the debate significantly.

After World War I, the victorious powers, namely the USA and the UK, agreed that war, a legitimate tool of conflict resolution, was catastrophic in its consequences and should therefore be avoided at all costs. This consensus, the idealist tradition, held that international society was essentially social in character, with various norms and values creating a fundamentally moral context within which states act. Thus war was seen as the product of misunderstandings amongst potentially moral beings in an international society (Hollis and Smith, 1991).[4]

Realism in contrast, ushered in by the publication in 1939 of E.H. Carr's *The Twenty Years' Crisis, 1919–39*, challenged the idealist belief that politics could be the realization of ethics, and that an orderly international society of states could exist. Realists argued that states, unlike individuals, could not act in response to an abstract moral ideal; they were by their very sovereign nature destined to compete with all other states for power and security in an essentially anarchical international system. 'Anarchy' in this context refers to the absence of any supranational authority; that is, to the fact that there is no world government or sovereign power to monitor or regulate the behaviour of states.

A large volume of realist literature was therefore concerned with the causes and consequences of conflict in the international system, and specifically conflict amongst the great powers. When realism triumphed after World War II, the focus of IR became one of maintaining the external security (and in effect the sovereignty) of the state in the face of international anarchy. International politics was termed high (read: 'important') politics. In contrast domestic issues, such as development, were considered to be low politics and not the concern of IR. Realism thus made an explicit distinction between the international and the domestic, based on the presence or absence of sovereignty.

While economic processes are clearly related to state capacities, IR also made an explicit distinction between the economic and the political. IR was about politics. The question of development, on the other hand, was an economic one. Thus the lens through which IR viewed the world was one which highlighted the importance of international political concerns and did not therefore include the concerns of national economic development.

The focus on power and security[5] (see chapter 9) was given credence by the Cold War, which provided fodder for the growth of security or strategic studies. Framed in realist terminology, power became the means and the end by which the state survived. Importantly, the Cold War emerged at the same time as the process of decolonization was accelerating. This had implications for the manner in which the Third World was viewed.

Historically, most of the Third World was incorporated into large empires and was studied as part of colonial policy, mainly through international history. Independence struggles were approached from the point of view of how to devolve power peacefully, the potential effects of the loss of empire, or the study of those politicians who paved the way for decolonization. International history was written from the more powerful nations' point of view.

The emerging Third World states were not major power players. Reason dictated that those states which had no influence on (power in) the international system were not the focus of IR. Instead the Third World became a matter of foreign policy concern; a place where Communism must be contained. Crisis in the Third World was recognized; the Vietnam War, the invasion of Grenada, the existence of Cuba, even the success of the Organization of Petroleum Exporting Countries (OPEC) have all been part of the study of IR. To the extent that the developing countries have presented a threat to international security, they have been watched and studied not so much for their own contribution to the extant international system, but as part of the wider concern for international order.

Finally, IR did not seek to be a discipline which concerned

itself with *normative* questions; that is, with questions about prescribed forms of conduct or with moral standards (Barry, 1981). Indeed in its recent past IR has sought to rid itself of its more normative tradition in idealism, believing that there is no room for morality between states (C. Brown, 1992). Realism claimed that international politics should be approached in a more rational and scientific manner, with careful analysis of the cause and effect of states' actions. Realism contended that the rights and duties of states did not go beyond political boundaries. Consequently questions about international justice, the distribution of resources between states, or the extent of poverty in the world could not properly be addressed (O. O'Neill, 1993, p. 308).

Political realism remains the predominant, but not the only, perspective in IR. It has greatly influenced the manner in which IR has evolved. Subsequent to the debate between idealism and realism there was another (less significant) debate between realism and behaviouralism.[6] Since the 1980s it has often been argued that there are three rival paradigms in IR: *realism/neo-realism, liberalism/pluralism* and *neo-Marxism*, each offering a different view of the world. The debate between these perspectives is termed the 'Inter-Paradigm' debate.

However, the three paradigms start from different assumptions about the nature of the international system, the character and significance of its units, and the processes at work.[7] Thus there is no objective means for choosing between them, and hence not much real debate (Hollis and Smith, 1991). Despite their incommensurability, both the liberal/pluralist and the neo-Marxist perspectives have challenged a number of realist assumptions and altered the focus of IR, so that questions of development (albeit in a limited form) have not been entirely excluded.

Briefly, the liberal/pluralist school of thought encompasses both *transnationalism* – that is, the claim that the state is no longer the dominant actor in the international system but is challenged by other, non-state actors – and *interdependence* – that is, the belief that increasing links between national economies make states more vulnerable to events in other parts of the world (Keohane and Nye, 1977). The existence of other actors and their activities in various spheres means that power no longer resides in states alone, and that the national (or state) interest becomes difficult to define or identify. The transnational approach points to new types of actors and activities, which changes the nature of international relations from interstate relations to a more multifocal approach. The interdependence perspective claims that increased trade, investment and technology linkages lead to increased vulnerability and sensitivity between actors. IR thus becomes a function of economic linkages as well as of world politics.

The liberal/pluralist perspective has held a certain appeal for the Third World because it seems to imply that all states are linked by their mutual vulnerability. No longer, as in realism, are weak states unimportant; interdependence implies there is a mutuality of interests between the North and the South. Thus in 1974, the call for a new international economic order (NIEO) argued that changes in the global economic order which would help to develop the Third World were essential for the future progress of the whole world. However, interdependence, as it was conceived, applied only to the North. Some states (in the North) were more equally interdependent than others (in the South). The NIEO was in effect stillborn, and the South quickly lost faith in the myth of the universality of interdependence. (For more discussion of the NIEO, see chapter 7.)

The Marxist tradition has traditionally only occupied a small part of IR. It was revitalized in the nineteenth century through the study of imperialism, but was ignored again by mainstream IR until the 1970s. The neo-Marxist tradition which emerged out of Latin America in the 1950s, provided an analysis of a capitalist world economy which incorporates an industrialized centre, or core, and an underdeveloped periphery. In this sense, by including the periphery in its analysis, it is more 'international' than the other paradigms have been.

The neo-Marxist or *dependency* paradigm became for scholars in Latin America, the Caribbean and Africa, as well as Marxists scholars in the West, the theoretical and ideological perspective through which they viewed the world. At its heart was the question of development; that is, how best and under what conditions development can occur, and what the obstacles to development are. The catalyst for interest in neo-Marxism by IR scholars was provided by the confrontational nature of North–South relations in the 1970s and its impact on the international system. However, since then neo-Marxist approaches have tended to be depicted as fringe elements of the discipline (Olson and Groom, 1991). Although the neo-Marxist paradigm is recognized, and listed (Korany, 1986), it is not used to explain phenomena. This may in part be due to the deficiencies of the paradigm in terms of its explanatory potential (and this will be explored later). However, it is also a result of the discipline being seen through the lens of the hegemonic powers and their concerns. Consequently only relatively few IR scholars have grappled with the question of development.

Thus it is possible to argue that the manner in which the discipline of IR has been constructed has made it inhospitable to engaging with questions of development, in particular in the Third World. There is in effect an institutionalized inertia in traditional IR which discourages research on the question of development.

What can the question of development contribute to IR?

Implicit in the term 'development' is some degree of teleology; that is, it implies a process of change and transformation in a particular, purposeful direction. As a starting point we shall assume development to be *an on-going process of qualitatively ameliorated social, political and economic change* – that is, progressive change which improves and sustains the quality of life of human society. (The means by which this will be achieved does not concern us immediately.) This definition does not assume a single specified end point; the act of development is an on-going process (rather than a stage).

If we ask whether the process is the same for all societies, the answer must be negative. Nor is it the same in all historical periods. Different temporal and cultural environments make possible different development outcomes. This should not imply that there is no value in comparative studies of development policy and practice. Comparative studies help us to make sense of, or organize, processes which have enough in common to make their differences significant. Even if particular development experiences appear to be unique, we can only understand them as such with reference to other experiences of development.

The way we decide what constitutes meaningful development will necessarily include some element of subjective choice. Anthropologists argue about whether tribal societies should be left in their traditional state or be given the benefits of civilization as we know it. Conservatives, in general, argue that traditional society is necessarily good because it upholds tested values. Yet societies do change, through internal dynamism and external responses, and what we seek to understand when studying development is the nature of these changes and the forces which influence them.

Development studies, as a field of enquiry, has sought to examine (national) development processes and to formulate theories of development. It has focused on the Third World and in particular on issues of poverty, inequality and growth within these states. It is thus very much problem-oriented, dealing with questions of how to achieve increases in national income or improvements in the quality of life. While IR has sought to describe the world as it is, the study of development is explicitly normative. It not only seeks to explain, but also embodies, certain ideas about what development should mean and seeks to effect the desired changes. Like IR it is multidisciplinary, drawing insights from a variety of fields including economics, anthropology, politics and history. The result is an increasingly complex and open-ended discipline.

Following Hettne (1995a), it is possible to identify three main categories of development theory. The first, *European* (or *orthodox*) development theory, is based on the idea of the replicability of the European experience (in particular the necessity of industrialization) in the former colonies. It assumes that development is an automatic process if the right preconditions exist. It also assumes that development follows a specific and universally applicable path, ultimately arriving at the point of modernity. This theory does not deal with the specificity of development in the periphery.

The second category of theories is largely *structuralist* in its orientation, focusing on the global structure of capitalism. Importantly, these theories originate in the Third World, and are explicitly concerned to make the development experience relevant and indigenous. In this category one would find the neo-Marxist/dependency paradigm adopted by IR. Here (in its extreme variants) explanations for the lack of development are assumed to be the logical outcome of the structure of the world economy, which is divided into core and periphery. The periphery (the Third World) consists of weak and vulnerable actors, and there is little that can be done about this.

Finally, and more recently, dissatisfaction with the whole development discourse has led to what may be called an *anti-modernist* school of thought. The proponents of this group argue that 'the idea of development stands like a ruin in the intellectual landscape' (W. Sachs, 1992, p. 1), and that it is necessary to get rid of the whole Western-inspired debate and create 'another' development in order to deal with, for example, the environmental crisis (see chapter 5).

It would be difficult to identify any single theory as being dominant in the current literature, although the resurgence of orthodox (European/Western) theory, in the guise of *neo-liberalism* (see chapter 3), is increasingly pervasive. However, there is also an increasing interest in the diversity of development experience and comparative research. This can be attributed to a number of factors, not least the increasing diversity of the Third World itself, which presents a challenge to a discipline that has too often made inappropriate generalizations.

First, incorporating the question of development in IR demands an approach which recognizes the interaction between the economic and the political. Although the study of development was initially (in European development theory) concerned with economic growth, and indeed its preoccupation with economic indicators remains, it was soon recognized that development is a multidimensional process, and that the links between the economic and the political were important. Thus *political economy of development* (PED) approaches emerged (Hettne, 1995a) which, it can be argued, tie in with *international political economy* (IPE) approaches within IR. IPE examines the links between the economic and the political, as well as the national and the international.[8] It may be that the most fruitful link between development and IR lies in creating a (new) global political economy of development (see chapter 9). The word 'new' is used because the current IPE has, through its focus on power, consigned the question of development to the periphery. There are elements of a new IPE already, best exemplified in Murphy and Tooze (1991).

Secondly, I have pointed out that development studies is

explicitly normative. Although it is concerned with disparities of material resources and the social consequences of this in different societies, academics and practitioners engaged in development want not only to analyse and observe the world, but also to prescribe change. IR in contrast has sought to deny its normative underpinning (although it is now trying to reclaim it) through its positivist stress on scientific, value-free observations. A normative element would, in general, argue that either political communities or humanity as a whole had an obligation (derived from a multitude of sources) to act upon the knowledge of the existence of widespread and unnecessary poverty. We would thus be engaging in debates which have preoccupied moral philosophers for a long time, but which have equal relevance to the study of the international system.

Thirdly, the question of development in IR would contribute to a more globally focused and holistic approach in IR, the subject of which is the whole of humanity rather than just a small, powerful and wealthy sector. Development cannot be assumed to be a localized or national problem. That is, unless it is possible to isolate a particular country completely from the international system, and to understand its economic, political and social system without reference to the global environment (historical or contemporary), development remains in theory a global issue. It links the idea of national development to the global context.

Finally, it is increasingly clear that questions of change and transformation are no longer (if they ever were) important only to the Third World.[9] Increasingly, post-industrial and post-communist societies are grappling with the questions of how to maintain levels of growth and employment, and are using development theory. It seems as though the tables have turned.

Development in a global context

IR has not grappled with the question of development, for a variety of reasons mentioned in the first section of this chapter. The question therefore remains as to how IR might incorporate the question of development within its ambit.

One of the current debates in IR is between positivist and post-positivist theory (S. Smith, 1995). The rather wide post-positivist grouping encompasses what has become known as *critical theory*. This sees theory as being constitutive of the reality it seeks to explain. That is, it argues that we cannot see the social world in an objective, value-free way. However, it does not want to go the way of being completely relativist and claiming that all reality is a social construction imposed unwittingly on the world. Critical theory therefore argues that it is possible to judge between rival truth claims. The main, but not the only, criterion for doing so lies in whether the theory is emancipatory (seeking to better the human condition) or whether it merely wants to take the world as it is and describe it. The difficulty with this is of course raised by the question: emancipation for whom? Is there an objective criterion for defining emancipation?

Nevertheless, critical theory replaces problem-solving, positivist theory (realism et al.), which takes an objective view of knowledge, with theory which is aware of the interests it represents and those it excludes. It thus embodies a self-reflective capacity. This is certainly needed, and is increasingly becoming a part of IR, and in particular of the new IPE tradition (Murphy and Tooze, 1991). This, it is argued, is the first step towards the inclusion of the question of development in IR.

The second step would be for IR to steer away from its desire (like development economics) to be value-free and scientific in its understanding of the social world and so to rid itself of moral responsibility. This is not to deny that there are moral assumptions in IR, but to say that any notions of global responsibility or international justice are tempered, if not curtailed, by principles of sovereignty and non-intervention.

The principle of state sovereignty creates political communities with few obligations to each other. It assumes that states are independent entities and that each is responsible for matters which are essentially within its territorial jurisdiction.[10] Thus there is a tension between questions of international justice and how this can be practically realized within the constraints of the principles of sovereignty.

The debate becomes more complex if we argue for the historical specificity of development; that is, that there can be no single idea of development universally applicable for all societies. Instead the particular traditions and cultural practices of a community must be recognized as valid. By this account there can be no assertion that, for example, what we understand as discrimination against women should be reduced in the development process because it is recognized to be unjust.

O. O'Neill (1993), in talking about justice, highlights two main types. The first consists of idealized accounts of justice which stress the need to abstract from the particularities of political communities. Justice would thereby be blind to those particularities. The second is a relativized account of justice which acknowledges the variety and differences among political communities. Principles of justice would therefore be grounded in the discourse of particular (actual) communities, and consequently national boundaries would become the limits of justice.

Either account is problematic on its own. Although idealized approaches would give the appearance of justice being impartial between weak and strong states, in fact they might legitimate a particular account of justice which suited some actors more than others. For example, the human rights discourse is put forward as universal, but may reflect a Western world view; and industrialization has been put forward as the best means of development, yet it clearly helps some groups in society more than others. Thus what we assume to be universal may in fact be particular.

On the other hand, relativized accounts of justice demand that context be taken into account, and so may endorse practices of sexism or discrimination. The dilemma is this: 'while relativist approaches are uncritical of established privilege, idealised approaches are uncritical of the privilege from which they abstract' (O. O'Neill, 1993, p. 304).

O'Neill thus argues for an account of justice which meets the demand for universal principles but which can be effected with contextualized judgements. Thus abstract principles will guide contextualized judgements without lapsing into relativism. The logical outcome of this is, however, that one can only ever make minimal moral claims, because there are few such universal principles. Nevertheless, this represents a valid starting point for debates about what constitutes development (are there any universal ideals?) and what obligations the international community has to effect it.

The chapter began with the claim that IR is by definition constructed at the level of the international. Most theories in IR have some conception of an international system, and this, whatever its character, provides the framework within which development takes place. The reality in the 1990s is of an incredibly complex and yet emerging system. What is needed is the adoption of an approach which looks at questions of change and transformation in the global context, but with due attention to the specificity of different societies and cultures. Thus the study of development in IR would not simply be of 'national development', nor would it be of the sum of the different national developments of a particular group of countries. Indeed Dower (1994) argues that 'there is no reason at all why the unit of development thinking must be the nation state, and every reason to recognise a whole range of units or levels of thinking about development, from that of local communities to that of the whole world as the appropriate unit of development'.

The interplay between the system and its units would be important. In what ways could the units change the system and in what ways would the system determine the extent of change possible?[11] Development in IR would therefore focus on different societies, at different stages of development, as they attempted to improve their individual or collective position in the global political economy.

The task is to develop approaches which can explain the increasing divergence, point towards a means of extracting useful general principles from this, and incorporate the multitude of options open to the different units (even within a capitalist world economy) in any new analyses and policies. The remainder of this book is an attempt to sketch out what I consider to be some of the most important policy areas and issues facing the commonly marginalized regions of the world in the 1990s. These areas and issues are important not only because they refer to the different dimensions of the development question, but also because they involve a rethinking of traditional relationships between the three worlds, and challenge the assumption of a homogeneous Third World and all the generalizations which go with it.

Summary

The basic argument of this chapter builds on the premise that the study of development has been relatively neglected in modern IR. This neglect stems in part from the manner in which IR, the discipline, has been constructed. It is argued that the question of development can contribute to the creation of a more reflective and inclusive discipline which is global in scope. However, it is not possible to simply add development to the current ingredients and hope to come up with a perfect recipe. What would be needed is the creation of a new global political economy of development which takes account of the specificity of development in a changing global system, and which steers towards more critical and normative approaches.

2 A Question of Terminology

Introduction

'Development occupies the centre of an incredibly powerful semantic constellation. There is nothing in modern mentality comparable to it as a force guiding thought and behaviour. At the same time, very few words are as feeble, as fragile, as incapable of giving substance and meaning to thought and behaviour as this one' (Esteva, 1992, p. 8). The concept of development is, like that of IR, ambiguous. It can refer to the process of developing, as well as the end state. In the social sciences the question of development presupposes a particular group of states (or region) within which the act of development will take place (or be imposed). That is, it refers not so much to the obvious – that all states are in an on-going process of change and transformation – as to a specific group of states defined as lacking or needing 'development'.

However, this terminology is significant because, in defining a particular group of states as 'developing', it immediately implies a need to develop these states, to enable them to catch up – and so the development discourse was born. The language used to describe particular phenomena or practices can have an important effect on the subject of enquiry as well as the manner in which it is approached. We therefore need to recognize the values embodied in the language we use. If we take meanings for granted, or fail to explore them critically, then the analytical capacity of our work will be lessened.

There are a number of categories or classifications used to

group different states together. The criteria used tend to be levels of economic, political or cultural achievement, or some combination thereof. This chapter queries whether the terms in use are in fact appropriate categories, and/or whether, in the light of the contemporary international system, we need to reconsider taken-for-granted concepts. Is there an appropriate or adequate means of classification which can make sense of an increasingly complex reality?

Classificatory schemas

In the world of states, a distinction is made between the *developing* and the *developed* states. At a very general level the developed states include Western Europe, Northern America, Japan, Australia, New Zealand and a few others. The developing states are those of Latin America, the Caribbean, Africa and Asia. This distinction is based on a variety of objective social and economic criteria. For example, developing states tend to have a high incidence of absolute poverty, low life expectancy, high infant mortality, low levels of adult literacy, and heavy reliance on primary commodity exports. Developed states tend to be industrialized and to have a large service sector, and the populace lead longer and healthier lives. There are of course always exceptions to any such generalizations.

Often the developing states are referred to as *less developed* or *underdeveloped*. From the criteria listed above it is easy to see that developing, underdeveloped and less developed states are the antithesis of the developed. These terms posit a dichotomy between those states which are assumed to be at a higher stage (even the end) of development, and those which are lacking in development. The terms derive largely from European or orthodox theories, which assume that development is a linear trajectory from a backward hinterland to a progressive metropolis (Rostow, 1960). They imply the lack of, and consequent need for, development, progress and modernization. If we adopt a more critical perspective it is possible to see that, by accepting these opposites as unproblematic, we perpetuate the acceptance of the 'developed' state (that is, the Western state) as superior, the ultimate reference point, and implicitly adopt a Eurocentric perspective.

The World Bank uses economic criteria to categorize countries. In its annual *World Development Report* the main criterion
for classification is gross national product (GNP) per capita. The
categories are as follows:

1 Low-income economies are those with a per capita GNP of
less than $725 in 1994.
2 Middle-income economies are those with a per capita GNP of
between $726 and $8,995 in 1994. This category is further subdivided into lower middle-income and upper middle-income
economies.
3 High-income economies are those with a per capita GNP of
more than $8,995 in 1994 (World Bank, 1996).

This classification focuses exclusively on empirical, quantitative criteria and therefore is subject to the criticism that development can never be understood by an analysis of purely economic
phenomena. Indeed the World Bank recognizes this and states
that 'classification by income does not necessarily reflect development status' (World Bank, 1994), yet it presents no further
explanation of development. Because it is 'The World Bank',
and because it regularly publishes reliable data, the Bank's use
of GNP per capita has a legitimating effect; it is assumed that
GNP per capita is a reliable and accurate measure of development.

There are well-known problems with relying on GNP per
capita as a measure even of economic development. First, GNP
is a gross measurement with no room for an analysis of income
distribution. It can thus mask extreme inequalities within a
given state. Second, it pays attention only to activities which are
visible, legitimate and paid. It does not account for productive
activity which is unpaid (housework) or illegal (prostitution) or
invisible (street vending), all of which can constitute a significant percentage of economic activity in many low-income economies.

The terms 'North' and 'South' are less well known and
emphasize the geographical fact of a northern, mainly industrialized hemisphere and southern, mainly primary-
commodity-producing states. Australia and New Zealand are
the major exceptions to this division, as they are considered to
be part of the North. The terms also have political significance.

In the 1970s the North/South dialogue rose to prominence with the OPEC price rises, a commodity price boom, the call for a NIEO, and later, the publication of the Brandt Report (1980). The OPEC action united the South, even the oil importers, against the North because the South saw the oil price rises as an example of how it could exercise commodity power over the North. OPEC's success was a godsend; 'it provided hope where previously there had been nothing but despair' (Thomas, 1987, p. 75). Indeed the OPEC success led to the proposal for an Integrated Programme for Commodities (IPC: see chapter 7) in an attempt to secure improved prices for a list of commodities. However, the intransigence of the North in respect of trade led to a change in strategy. The Brandt Report (1980), instead of being confrontational, argued that North and South were interdependent; poverty in the South would have a knock-on effect in the North, whereas if the North provided additional financial resources for the South, this would create a dynamic South with a greater demand for Northern products. While the idea of mutual self-interest was not convincing to the North, it was another rallying call for leaders in the South. The term 'South' thus became more widely used to indicate a political stand against widening economic disparities with the North.

While it is perhaps less value-laden than other distinctions, the North/South terminology also leaves many questions unanswered. Where, for example, does one place South Africa (with high levels of industrialization) or Portugal (with a large, relatively poor rural sector)? More recently, the rise of the NIEs as major industrial producers (see chapter 4) challenges the perception of the South as a group of primary producers. The North/South distinction is also in danger of being used mainly as a geographical description rather than as an analysis of social, political and economic phenomena.

Another popular categorization is that of the *First*, *Second* and *Third Worlds*. The First World encompasses the industrialized West, the Second World the socialist bloc countries, and the Third World the newly independent states. Many critics of this terminology, on different sides of the political spectrum, have pointed out that the Third World has been invented as the direct result of the First World's activities, either through the creation of peripheral economies (Clapham, 1985) or through processes of economic assistance (Bauer, 1981). Thus it is argued that the

Third World has no existence outside of its relationship with the First World.

However, the term 'Third World' originally referred to those states which were excluded from power in an international system caught up in the post-World War II East–West rivalry (the Cold War). The author of the term, Alfred Sauvy (Hadjor, 1993), saw the Third World as having the revolutionary potential to fight against this exclusion. The term thus reflected both exclusion and aspiration and did not (originally) have the same connotations as 'backward' and 'underdeveloped'.

Initially rejected, the term gained popularity when more states became independent in the 1950s and 1960s, as referring to a path between state socialism and liberal capitalism; a third path. It was embraced in recognition of the fact that, as newly independent states, they shared a common history of colonialism and common problems as a result of this history. Thus neither capitalism nor socialism could be effected in the same manner in the Third World, but would take on different characteristics.

Is the Third World a useful concept?

What differentiates the Third World from other states and makes it a useful category? First, there is the fact of colonialism. Characteristically the Third World countries have been colonies of the First and sometimes the Second World (although it is also possible to argue that imperialism existed even within the Second World). Notable exceptions are the USA, Canada and Australia, which are all former colonies of Britain and part of the First World. The observation is significant nevertheless, because it tells us that there has been (and still is) an integral connection between the groups through colonialism, which has helped establish the extant international division of labour.

The implications of colonialism are too many to cover here. However, one important problem facing many Third World states after independence has been how to forge a state which can claim political authority over the populace and, inextricably linked to this, how to use public power and authority to improve the quality of life of the population (Manor, 1991). Often it has proved difficult to combine the need for legitimacy with real social and economic development. While it may be true that all states face this dilemma (indeed it is a constantly recurring theme of political economy), and it should not be assumed that the state in Africa, Asia and Latin America is simply a product of colonialism (Bayart, 1991), the serious ruptures caused by colonialism to any pre-existing forms of government have meant that the problem of nation building has occupied a large part of the state's activities after independence. This is further exacerbated in those countries where questions of survival, for example due to famine or disease, preponderate over questions of development.

Another important defining factor, embodied in the original use of the term, is that of lack of power (Strange, 1988), often cited as peripherality (Clapham, 1985), vulnerability and relative weakness (Krasner, 1985; Thomas, 1987) or dependency (Dos Santos, 1973). This implies not only external reliance, but an inability to set agendas or determine outcomes in the global arena. The lack of power determines, to a large extent, the role and place of the state in the international system. It thus points to the external or international context within which states act.

Third, the term 'Third World' refers to a self-defined group of states. It is embraced by those states represented in the UN by the Group of 77 (G77, now numbering 126). It is used as a political bargaining tool in recognition of the fact that as individual states they cannot command significant power, but collectively they are a force to be reckoned with in international forums. The ability of the G77 to outvote other members of the UN in the General Assembly has brought forth criticism from the USA. Indeed the USA have withdrawn funding from UNESCO because they feel it is a forum for radical Third World views.

Alongside World Bank categories and sub-categories of nations ranked according to per capita income is the principle of 'self-election'. This allows preferences within special trade arrangements to any state which chooses to define itself as a *less developed country* (LDC). In practice, all members of the G77 are recognized to be LDCs under most schemes. Interestingly this principle has created a reluctance on the part of the Third World to graduate from the status of LDC into an MDC (more developed country) or NIC (newly industrialized country), not so much because of the loss of preferential status as because of the damage to Third World solidarity which would result from the creation of hierarchies among LDCs (H. O'Neill, 1984).

However, the G77 is increasingly selective in its use of the political bargaining tool. Because the group is so large, it represents states which have different interests in areas of international policy making. Thus in more recent international negotiations on the environment it is possible to see where the interests of large, semi-industrial states such as India and China diverge from those of smaller, non-industrial states (see chapter 5), or, in the case of GATT, where the interests of food exporters differ from those of food importers (see chapter 7). Thus the demise of the Third World has been proclaimed.

The end of the Third World?

There are a number of problems with this categorization of states, which have led to its validity being reconsidered. One is the growing economic difference between Third World states. Hong Kong and Singapore have been classified as high-income countries by the World Bank since 1989, and over 50 per cent of exports from Brazil and Mexico are now manufactures, compared with an average of 24 per cent for Sub-Saharan Africa (World Bank, 1994). Economic differentiation has created a group of wealthy oil-producing states, the NICs and near NICs in Asia and South America, and states whose economies consistently experience negative growth rates. There is the emergence of a hierarchical structure even within the Third World.

Do the existence of the NICs and their phenomenal rates of growth and levels of income mean that the term has outgrown its origins? It would be absurd not to acknowledge and take account of the immense and growing differences among Third World states. The term 'Fourth World' has been used to subdivide part of the Third World into a new category of least developed or underdeveloping states. Like the term 'Third World', the idea of a Fourth World originated in France to describe structural marginalization within the advanced capitalist countries. It therefore highlights an important point: that questions of poverty and marginalization are not peculiar to the Third World but can be found in First World states as well. It does, however, in its acknowledgement of differentiation, point towards an awareness of the limited validity of the term 'Third World'.

We need to ask whether the traditional Cold War perception of an international system divided into three worlds has been destroyed by recent events. During the Cold War, the USA and the USSR competed for the allegiance of the Third World, promising the benefits of superior development to their supporters. The pawns were sacrificed, and when the game was over the world had changed, but the promise of development was never fulfilled.

Without a Cold War there is no conceptual meaning in the term 'Second World'. The dissolution of the Communist Bloc, the Council for Mutual Economic Assistance (Comecon), is a significant part of the transformations within the world order in the 1990s, yet Eastern Europe faces problems of a slightly different nature from the Third World. Any new terminology must take into account where this group of states will insert itself in the international system.

The term 'Third World' has been used to group together states which were never homogeneous, but have been placed in a category of undifferentiated poverty. Indeed the assumption of the Third World has been used to justify and perpetuate the belief in unilinear progress. It is thus caught up in a dialogue born of a desire to universalize that which is particular. Only by beginning from a position which is critical of these assumptions can we begin to understand the diversity of the group.

The term 'Third World' masks enormous historical, cultural, economic, social and political variations, which in themselves provide a challenge for the social sciences. It is important to recognize the immense generality of all such categorizations; there are always exceptions to any broad grouping. Using the term 'Third World' does not simplify the difficult task of understanding increasing diversity. But it is equally important not to deny the material reality of poverty. Africa, for example, has been described as 'the most unstable, most marginal, least productive, most debt distressed and most vulnerable region in the world. Despite Africa's abundant human and material resources, no country can be reasonably described as developed, developing or as a NIC' (Ihonvbere and Turner, 1993, p. 35).

Summary

The language of development is historically constructed in such a manner that it confers particular images of what developing, less developed and underdeveloped states lack. The concept of development has been used to prescribe a particular type of growth or evolution, which is assumed to be universally desirable and possible. These assumptions are at the very least questionable.

There are a number of alternative possible classifications, none of which is entirely satisfactory or makes sense of the complexity and heterogeneity that is the subject of development discourse. It is thus possible to conclude with Hettne and Korany that 'the hierarchy within the South is indeed in search of a theory' (Korany, 1986, quoted in Hettne, 1995a, p. 265) as well as a terminology. Likewise the so-called First World is increasingly differentiated and is not an unproblematic category. For now, we will use the term 'Third World', not as an analytical category or as a descriptive one (except in a very basic sense), but in its original sense (exclusion and aspiration) and because it describes a self-elected status, with the important caveat that few generalizations about Third World states are possible and specific studies are necessary.

3 | Theories of Development

Introduction

'The question of development' necessarily encompasses many different accounts of what constitutes meaningful development, and, logically following on from this, there are many contending theories. Chapter 1 pointed out that the study of development has most often focused on how to improve living conditions within a given state, or group of states, but that development cannot be considered to be a purely local (national) issue because it is not possible to isolate a particular state from the context of the international system. There are no completely autonomous states. Thus national development is intricately linked to the international sphere. The nature of these linkages, whether they are positive or negative, predetermined or open to manipulation, constitutes one of the most contentious issues among different theorists of development. This is one of the themes explored in this chapter.

Larrain (1989) argues that the evolution of theories of development has followed that of capitalism. Thus different phases of capitalism and the particular social formations it engendered gave rise to particular theories of development. Not only is development historically specific, but so too are theories of development. The comment is relevant when we consider the applicability to the 1990s of development theories written in the 1960s and 1970s. That is, does the nature of the international system today demand a historically specific analysis of the question of development in IR?

This chapter follows the chronological emergence of two main development perspectives: European development theory, in particular modernization theory, and the neo-Marxist or dependency perspective which emerged from the work of the Economic Commission for Latin America (ECLA). While the former tends to view the international environment as neutral (or positive), the latter is more critical of it. Yet few attempts at delinking from the international system have proved successful. The question remains one of what is the best way to be linked. The last part of the chapter looks at the changing global context within which theories of development must be rethought. Since the 1980s, neo-liberalism has been the predominant approach. Its pervasiveness must be set in the context of increasing globalization, which is transforming the international system and its constituent parts. The increasing diversity of the Third World seems to imply that no single paradigm is likely to provide a sufficient explanation.

European (orthodox) development theory

The idea of development was not originally applied to the Third World. Rather it was first used to refer to the struggle of the British bourgeoisie against the remnants of feudalism (Hettne, 1995). However, with the advent of capitalism in Europe, development was taken for granted, seen as a process which evolved almost automatically. The idea of development thus became applicable to pre-capitalist societies – the newly independent countries in Latin America or the colonies of Europe.

Modernization theory is based largely on the transition from feudalism to capitalism in Europe. It explains development in the Third World in a similar fashion: as a transition between backwardness and modernity. All states are assumed to follow the same evolutionary path, mimicking that of the already industrialized ones, by the diffusion and adoption of the correct (capitalist) values, beliefs, institutions: 'Modernization theories, therefore, seek to identify in the organisation and/or history of industrial countries the social variables and institutional factors whose change was crucial for their process of development, in order to formulate the process for the newly developing countries' (Larrain, 1989, p. 87).

W. W. Rostow's *The Stages of Economic Growth* (1960) empha-
sized the economic determinants of the transition. According to
Rostow there are five successive historical stages through which
the backward societies must pass in order to become modern.
These were the traditional society, the preconditions for take-
off, the take-off, the road to maturity, and the age of high mass
consumption.

Traditional societies are mainly agricultural and characterized
by low productivity. The second stage, the *preconditions for take-
off*, is stimulated by intrusions from the more advanced societies. These normally take the form of technology transfers,
leading to an expansion in trade and consequent economic
growth. In addition it is assumed that a spurt in economic
growth will lead to the political constitution of a national
(independent) state capable of managing the economy. During
the period of *take-off*, growth becomes a permanent feature in the
economy. This is the key stage in the process, achieved by an
increase in the rate of capital investment. As this rate increases
in new industries, new (modern) techniques are incorporated
into agricultural production to make it more competitive. Growth
becomes automatic. The *road to modernity* is characterized by the
modernization of all factors of the economy with the use of new
technologies. *High mass consumption*, the final stage, is reached
when the whole economy is oriented towards the production of
consumer durables and services. In this period it becomes
possible to consider goals of social security and welfare provision. It is also characterized by an increase in military expenditure.

Two main criticisms of the Rostovian variety of modernization theory are relevant to this chapter. First, there is little real
analysis of the international system and consequently of changes
in it. Second, the model conceptualizes the Third World as a
homogeneous mass and so cannot take account of diversity and
its consequences.

Rostow's model tends to assume that development is simple
equation; with the right inputs, the correct outcomes are possible. Development is thus a basically endogenous process; that
is, growing from within. There is no real analysis of the nature
of the international system and how it might determine the
potential and the capability for development at different
historical periods. While Rostow does recognize the difference

between late developers (the Third World) and early industrial economies, he argues that the former colonies are facilitated in their development by having access to already developed technology, for example medicine to lower infant mortality and improve the quality of life. Thus the Third World has the advantage of the presence of an already industrialized group of countries in the international system which can diffuse the right values and institutions.

Rostow does not acknowledge diversity in the Third World because he is writing in the context of a particular political agenda. The book is subtitled *A Non-Communist Manifesto*, and he writes firmly in the tradition of opposing the claim that Marxism presented the best way for the newly independent states to become incorporated into the modern world (Valenzuela and Valenzuela, 1981, p. 15). The model is assumed to apply to all traditional societies. There is no real examination of their particular nature (indeed, 'traditional' only refers to the absence of modernity) and how this might result in differing outcomes. In attempting to create a universal model, modernization underestimates the diversity of the Third World.

Modernization theories dominated the social sciences in the 1950s and 1960s, but the critique from the Third World was severe (Frank, 1969; Roxborough, 1979). Modernization theory was popular in the West because it confirmed suspicions and prejudices about backward societies and echoed paternalistic attitudes. Indeed it created the rationale for economic aid. The debate is still far from dead. Modernization theory resurfaces in current debates about modernity and post-modernity and in the neo-liberal agenda.

The Economic Commission for Latin America (ECLA)

ECLA was created by the UN in 1948 to examine the potential for economic development in Latin America. It was ECLA which levelled the first criticisms against modernization theory by arguing against the endogenous view of development in favour of a world dimension to all economic processes. ECLA posited the existence of a world system composed of a developed centre or core and an underdeveloped periphery. Raul Prebisch, who

chaired the commission, argued that the obstacles to development in the periphery lay not in the lack of entrepreneurial spirit
or the right values and attitudes, but in the nature of the
international system.

ECLA's analysis focused in particular on the nature of international trade. ECLA argued that the *terms of trade* for raw
materials were constantly decreasing relative to those for manufactures – that is, the prices paid for raw materials were lessen-
ing relatively. A continued decrease in the terms of trade for a
given product would negate any of the supposed benefits of
comparative advantage.[1]

ECLA argued that the terms of trade for raw materials declined for a number of reasons. First, raw materials were undervalued by the market, while manufactures were overvalued.
Second, the demand for raw materials decreases as incomes
increase, with consumers spending their increased income on
more refined products. Third, surplus labour in the periphery
pushes down wages and consequently the price of raw materials. Where labour is scarce (in the centre), wages are high and
consequently the prices for industrial products are high.

It follows that the periphery has to export increasing quantities of raw materials in order to continue to import the same
amount of industrial goods. Those states which produce industrial goods will grow faster than those which produce raw
materials and a widening gap between the centre and the
periphery will develop. This is the first theory of *unequal exchange*, which is developed later by Emmanuel (1972) and S.
Amin (1976) and reflects the negative view of the international
system which ECLA held.

ECLA suggested that the way forward for Latin America was
to reduce imports of manufactured goods through a process of
inward-oriented development known as import substitution
industrialization (ISI). ISI involves the substitution of foreign
manufactured imports with locally produced manufactures. In
this process tariffs are essential to protect infant industries from
competition with the already industrialized countries. The state
thus plays a significant role in planning and organizing the
industrialization process. ISI was to be facilitated by foreign
capital used to purchase imported capital goods. ECLA did not
question the assumption that development would take place
within capitalism. Indeed in seeking (like Rostow) to reject

Marxism, ECLA incorporated the belief that capitalist development is possible in the periphery, but through inward-oriented
policies.

By the 1960s, ECLA's analysis and prescriptions were under
heavy criticism, in particular from liberal political economists.
They claimed that the method used for ECLA's overwhelmingly
negative analysis of the international system, exemplified in the
'terms of trade' argument, was flawed. They pointed out that the
study of data from a limited period in history ignores the cyclical
nature of trade over time; that is, the tendency for trade to grow
and then contract in long or short cycles. The distinction between cycles and a constant deterioration in the terms of trade
is not made by ECLA.

Also, all raw materials do not follow the same pattern. Oil, for
example, is a high-priced raw material with a demand which is
fairly unresponsive to changes in price; hence the severe impact
of oil price rises. Indeed evidence seemed to suggest that there
was no overall, long-term sectorial decline in commodity prices,
and furthermore that short-term fluctuations in some commodities were not necessarily harmful. Thus Spraos (1980, p. 216)
concludes that 'while the deteriorating tendency cannot be
decisively refuted, it is open to doubt when the record up to the
1970s is taken into account'. (See chapter 7.)

Moreover, it was argued that the international market is more
flexible and responsive than the theory allows for, and indeed
that those states engaging with the market had benefited from
it. In contrast, the state in Latin America had overprotected the
industrial sector. The industries created behind protectionist
barriers tended to be inefficient, so that while ISI did encourage
industrialization, it did so at great cost. The need for raw
materials and capital goods to facilitate ISI led to excessive
borrowing and consequent balance of payment (BOP) deficits.
This in turn provoked the need for more foreign aid and loans.
ISI did not therefore reduce external vulnerability, it merely
changed the nature of it.

There were also criticisms from within the Third World,
focusing mainly on the domestic costs of ISI. Perhaps one of the
most often criticized consequences was the role of foreign
capital, which was supposed to be temporary and facilitating,
but became in effect a permanent necessity as BOP crises arose.
It was argued that the development of a manufacturing sector

took resources out of the agricultural export sector, which could, if investment had taken place, have provided the necessary foreign exchange.

Another relevant criticism is that ECLA, like modernization theory, did not look closely at the nature of society in Latin America, which would constrain or create particular types of development. For example, the policy of capital-intensive in-dustrialization produced more unemployment in countries where it was already high. ISI created an enclave economy; a small, privileged group of people with high incomes based on the new industries amidst a large, impoverished, urban labour force. In the process greater inequality in incomes was created within the urban sector as well as between the agricultural labour force and the industrial labour force.

The dependency perspective

While the dependency perspective criticizes the liberal assump-tions of ECLA, it has at the same time made use of ECLA's analysis of the international system. The existence of a centre and a periphery is the starting point for a number of writers who are united in their focus on peripheral economies and the effect external factors have on the internal structures of these eco-nomies (Larrain, 1989). Within the dependency perspective there are many diverse strands, a fact which is often glossed over by its critics.[2] This section examines the Frankian type of analy-sis, which sees little or no possibility of development for the periphery within a capitalist world system, and analyses which view qualified development as possible, even within capitalism. Both strands are united in their assumption that the world system is basically a capitalist one. Thus the questions they ask are about the potential (or not) for development within capitalism.

The development of underdevelopment thesis

Andre Gunder Frank (1969), one of the earliest and best-known dependency writers, criticizes the assumption of both European development theory and ECLA that capitalism is a liberating force. Frank argues instead that capitalism is to blame for the underdevelopment of Latin America. Capitalism, through imperialism, has expanded since the sixteenth century to incorporate the whole world in a single international system. This capitalist world system is made up of centres (metropolises) and peripheries (satellites) which are closely connected through social, political and economic structures. The centre consistently and systematically expropriates the economic surplus from the periphery through the mechanisms of the international market. This process produces simultaneously development in the centre and underdevelopment in the periphery: 'Development and underdevelopment each cause and are caused by the other in the total development of capitalism' (Frank, 1969, p. 240).

Frank argues that the weaker the ties between the two, the greater the possibility of autonomous development in the periphery, and the stronger the ties, the more the underdevelopment. Underdevelopment is not a stage, or a phase before development as posited by modernization theories, but a process which has been created by the situation of dependency and exists alongside development. According to Frank, capitalism must be abolished; development is only possible through delinking and establishing an autonomous (socialist?) system.

An important distinction should be made here about the meaning of the term 'dependency'. All states are to one degree or another dependent. For example, when two states trade, each economy becomes open to the vagaries of the other. By this definition, 'dependent' simply implies 'externally reliant'. But the dependency writers had something more in mind. T. Dos Santos (1970, p. 231) describes dependency as:

> a conditioning situation in which the economies of one group of countries are conditioned by the development and expansion of others. A relationship of interdependence between two or more economies or between such economies and the world trading system becomes a dependent relationship when some countries can expand through self impulsion while others, being in a dependent position, can only expand as a reflection of the expansion of the dominant countries, which may have positive or negative effects on their immediate development.

The distinction is important, because it highlights the claim of dependency writers that there is a qualitative difference between dependence amongst and between the centre, and the dependency of the centre on the periphery.

Frank presents a totalizing view of a single capitalist system. Following ECLA, trade is the mechanism of incorporation into this system and the source of exploitation through unequal exchange. But, contrary to ECLA's analysis, Frank sees no possibility of real development for the periphery within the system. The dependency of the periphery thus necessarily brings about underdevelopment. Frank, like modernization theorists before him, treats dependent societies as a general category, rather than looking at their historical specificity. Thus external relations always produce the same internal distortions in this model. There are no specific historical determinants which differentiate the response of different states to the same system.

Nevertheless, the idea of dependency challenged the Eurocentric bias of previous theories of development. It was soon adopted by Third World intellectuals outside Latin America, for example in the Caribbean and Africa, where the Frankian model was adapted to the peculiarities of their newly independent status. We will now briefly look at two variants, one from the Caribbean (the *plantation school*) and the other from Africa.

The plantation school Caribbean political economy has tended to follow the argument that close links with the world economy, in particular through the slave economy, have resulted in underdevelopment. However, the analysis is of specifically Caribbean situations of underdevelopment. Beckford (1972) looks at the phenomenon of persistent underdevelopment in the *plantation economies* of the world. These are economies that depend on the export of one or two primary commodities, and in which the plantation is the dominant social and economic institution. They are located mainly in the Caribbean, Latin America and parts of Asia. These economies have been exposed to 'modern' influences (the plantation is historically often foreign-owned) but at the same time remain underdeveloped, thus disproving the modernization thesis. Beckford argues that underdevelopment results from the institutional environment of the plantation and the nature of the economic, social and political organization which it engenders. He is seeking not to make any generalizations about all of the Third World but to analyse particular societies whose economies have been based largely on the plantation. Beckford is specifically concerned with development which improves the welfare of the population; while material advancement is important, even desirable, development must take account of the quality of life.

Small Garden, Bitter Weed (Beckford and Witter, 1982) provides a neo-Marxist analysis of society in the Caribbean. Beckford and Witter argue that the Caribbean has been exploited since colonialism, although the nature of exploitation may have changed. They seek to provide 'the kind of political educational ammunition to launch a final assault to eradicate the bitter weed of capitalism/imperialism once and for all' (Beckford and Witter, 1982, p. xviii). The ultimate aim, following Frank, is to build a socialist society rooted in the cultural tradition of the people of the Caribbean.

African dependency African theories of development also tend to be adapted from a Frankian type of analysis. African dependency writers argue that Africa was underdeveloped through its incorporation into the world capitalist system (Rodney, 1972),[3] so that 'autocentric and autodynamic development never became possible' (S. Amin, 1976, p. 292). African economies can only respond to developments in the centre. Whereas there, growth may imply development, this is not the case in the periphery where the development of underdevelopment takes place. Internally this creates an unequal society, with a local capitalist or bourgeois class and a subordinated mass of impoverished people. In addition, the capitalist class in the centre exploits the capitalist class in the periphery.

The solutions to this disarticulated type of uneven development are varied (Ofuatey-Kodjoe, 1991); some argue for strategies of self-reliance and regional integration, others for African socialism. The claim that the international system is inherently exploitative remains fundamental.

Dependency and development

The second group of dependency writers, typified by Cardoso and Faletto (1979), move away from the grand theory of Frank and Dos Santos and focus instead on historical studies of particular situations of dependency. Dependency, they argue, is not a blanket concept which explains situations of underdevelopment in all of the Third World. While the international system may be common to all states, the response to it by the Third World is not. There is something specific about the way in which the internal conditions of a given state react or interact with the international system. Thus similarly situated states frequently pursue different policies in response to external pressures (Haggard, 1990). This creates in some cases *dependent capitalist development* or *associated dependent development*, and in others stagnation. Dependency is not a sufficient condition for underdevelopment, but a conditioning situation mediated and altered through internal class formations and alliances, which produce a number of possible outcomes.

Cardoso and Faletto combine classical Marxist concepts of capitalist societies with new analyses of the specificity of development in dependent societies. While dependency is part and parcel of capitalism, its specific nature is determined by the way capitalism is received, opposed and modified internally. They thus reject the claim that dependency is purely externally caused and look instead at the 'historical transformation of structures by conflict, social movements and class struggles' (Cardoso and Faletto, 1979, p. x).

If capitalism does not produce the same changes or situations in the whole of the Third World, but differs according to local specificities of state and society, it follows that there must be different forms of dependent situations. Some, for example, produce development which is sustained by foreign capital, such as ISI. While there may be wealth with poverty, and growth alongside marginalization, this does not mean it is not development; just that it is a specific form of development.

This analysis necessarily leads to the question of whether it is merely a retrospective description of development in Latin America or whether there are any general conclusions to be drawn. A number of dependency writers carried out empirical investigations into specific development processes in Latin America. On the whole they arrived at few generalizable conclusions. The reasons for the lack of development in different states range from the control of national assets by foreign transnational corporations (TNCs), or deterioration in the terms of trade over a particular period, to the lack of clear and consistent government policies.

Cardoso and Faletto wish to blur the distinction between growth and development (Larrain, 1989). Sunkel (1969) and Furtado (1963), however, argue that growth in some sectors is possible without real national development. Growth is a purely economic measurement, while development is defined in terms of social and political as well as economic factors, including the fulfilment of human potential and the satisfaction of basic needs. Industrialization as experienced by Latin America in the period of ISI was characterized by reasonable levels of economic growth but did not bring about self-sufficiency and development. Instead it was a vehicle for a new type of dependency characterized by the penetration of foreign capital and TNCs.

The critique

There are many criticisms of the dependency perspective, although they are often based on a simplistic understanding of it. However, some of the criticisms levelled by both the left and the right remain valid. Perhaps most significantly, the concept of dependency is attacked for being too abstract and totalizing to be meaningful. Dependency, it is argued, has become an idea which explains everything. It tends to produce a tautological argument: that poor countries are poor because they are dependent, and any characteristics they display are attributed to their dependence (Larrain, 1989, p. 177). The dependency perspective cannot therefore explain outcomes contrary to its theoretical expectations. Yet it is empirically possible to find that underdevelopment is not causally related to dependence and likewise that underdevelopment exists in fully industrialized countries.

In addition, if modernization theory argued that backwardness could be overcome from within, the dependency perspective (at least in its Frankian form) goes to the opposite extreme and argues that the causal factors of underdevelopment are mainly external. While the dependency perspective does admit some causal internal factors, the emphasis is on the harmful impact of the international system. This necessarily leads to the need to pursue autonomous (even autarchic) development policies. The former involves self-government or independence – that is, acting in accordance with one's own principles and laws

– while the latter implies economic self-sufficiency aimed at removing the need for imports. However, the call to delink from the international system has obvious empirical flaws. There have been few success stories among those countries which have delinked, not least because there is significant international pressure against it. The examples of Grenada and Cuba immediately spring to mind. While Cuba has achieved enormous success in terms of health and education, the economy is now rapidly deteriorating. The revolutionary New Jewel Movement in Grenada, on the other hand, was not given much of a chance by the international community before the island was invaded. The experience of the East Asian NIEs in embracing the international market appears to refute the dependency analysis. However, such a conclusion needs further scrutiny (see chapter 4).

The lack of a *theory* of development is also a glaring weakness. While dependency writers, even the dependent development writers, pointed out the obstacles to development, and sometimes the different manifestations of dependency, they did not formulate any new theory or programme for development which could be implemented once the obstacles were removed. In 1981 Frank wrote:

> the usefulness of . . . dependence theories of underdevelopment as guides to policy seems to have been undermined by the world crisis of the 1970s. The Achilles heel of these conceptions of dependence has always been the implicit, and sometimes explicit, notion of some sort of independent alternative for the Third World. This theoretical alternative never existed, in fact, certainly not on the non capitalist path and now apparently not even through socialist revolutions. The new crisis of real world development now renders such partial development and parochial dependence theories and policies invalid and inapplicable. (Frank, 1981, p. 27)

This from the father of dependency! Perhaps this points us towards an approach to development which recognizes a more complex link between the internal and the external, and can take account of the diversity of experience. However, before arriving at this point it is necessary to survey briefly the main competition to theories which argue for the specificity of development in the periphery: *liberal political economy* and its variant, *neo-liberalism*.

Liberal Political Economy

The liberal political economy (LPE) approach has become in effect the conventional or mainstream approach to development. This is due in part to the fact that the post-war international system has been fashioned on liberal values and assumptions. Consequently, the objective reality around us largely, but not totally, reflects this. It is also because, in the 1980s, neo-liberalism successfully challenged the welfare state in the North, and development theory in the South, to embrace the ideal of more liberal economic policy in a globalized market place. (Chapter 8 discusses the neo-liberal agenda further.)

The 1980s thus witnessed what has been called the counter-revolution in development theory and practice. (Importantly, the 1980s have also been referred to as the lost development decade for the Third World.) Neo-liberalism argued against two important ideas of development theory to date: that the Third World constituted a special case and should therefore have special concessions, policies and economic theories applied to it, and that the state should play a major role in economic development.

In contrast to the dependency perspective's pessimistic view of the international market, neo-liberalism argued that participation in the international market leads to the greatest good for the greatest number of people. In addition, this will happen only if the market is left alone, because it is essentially a self-regulating mechanism. Interference in the market and in the international division of labour[4] will serve only to reduce world trade and consequent harmony. This is a universal law, applying to all states at all times. There is consequently no room for Third World exceptions.

Thus the World Bank report on Africa in 1981 (the Berg Report) claimed that the constraints to development in Africa lay in its lack of human resources, overpopulation, political fragility, misguided policies and excessive state intervention. Development planning, ISI and state marketing boards had all failed to deliver the promised benefits. The report recommended the liberalization of trade, the promotion of exports and the reduction of state economic activity as a mechanism for increased economic growth and hence development.

In support of this the neo-liberals pointed out that the NIEs of

East Asia had, with their emphasis on profits, markets and trade, managed to achieve levels of growth which surpassed the First World's. The NIEs had clearly managed, by embracing the international market and new technologies, to alter their comparative advantage so that they became the most efficient producers of many industrial products. (LPE stipulates that countries should specialize in the production of those products in which they have a comparative advantage.)

Neo-liberalism thus argued that while the nature of the international system was important for development, it was not as important as dependency and other development theories argued. The problem was not the international market, but domestic policy which ignored market considerations. The practical implications of the neo-liberal thesis lay in its adoption by the Bretton Woods institutions – the World Bank and the International Monetary Fund (IMF) – in their policies of *structural adjustment*, downgrading previous concerns for policies to promote equity and poverty alleviation.

In ignoring, or consigning to a relatively minor role, the political (usually the state), neo-liberalism as applied to the Third World conveniently ignored the fact that markets can be and are manipulated by people, states and other economic actors so that some benefit by participation and others do not. While there are gains to be had from participation in a competitive framework of international specialization and trade, there are no mechanisms to ensure that all benefit equally, or even sufficiently. This dilemma does not disappear with the development of the global market place.

Globalization

What do we mean when we say the international system is becoming more global? The tendency towards a closely linked international system has previously been associated with theories of *interdependence* and *transnationalism*. Interdependence refers to 'situations characterised by reciprocal effects among countries or actors in different countries' (Keohane and Nye, 1977, p. 8), while transnationalism refers to the increased influence of non-state (mainly economic) actors across state boundaries.

Globalization is a concept much talked about, but perhaps undertheorized in IR (Hirst and Thompson, 1996). Certainly there is no single understanding of the idea. According to one author, globalization refers to 'the idea that, through a series of mechanisms, the world has become more closely interconnected, and by implication that it will continue to become more closely interconnected' (M. Smith, 1992, p. 253). The editors of the *Review of International Political Economy* (RIPE) define globalization as a qualitative change in the nature of social activities; linkages which are of an intensity never before experienced (A. Amin et al., 1994). Both understandings posit the idea that globalization is something relatively new and unique.

On the other hand, *world system* writers argue that there is nothing distinctive about the modern capitalist world system as it has developed since the sixteenth century (Frank, 1990). This highlights a more or less agreed point: that globalization represents a lengthy historical process, even within these different understandings.

It is important to ask what implications the empirical existence of globalization might have for development theory. One argument is that if the international system has changed significantly since the theories or approaches we have been discussing were formulated, then the context within which development theory and praxis take place will also have changed. This is said with the familiar caveat; the more things change, the more they stay the same. There are still stronger and weaker states, there is still marginalization and poverty, even though the form and place may well have changed. The question thus becomes: what does globalization imply for the national development prospects of different states, and, following on from this, in what sense can we talk about international or world development?

The globalization thesis is based on two significant processes. First, the role of the state has fundamentally changed. In the words of one author, it is now less of a civil association and more of an enterprise association (Cerny, 1994). What this means is that its main focus is the promotion of competitive economic activities at home and abroad. Consequently, 'confrontation in political life is reduced to questions concerning the comparative efficiency of alternative strategies for accommodating the interests of economic forces, and to a lesser extent for distributing the monetary benefits which their activities imply' (Scott, 1995, p. 2).

The state is less concerned with matters of domestic polity (democracy, social policy) and more with economic activities; that is, with becoming competitive in the international system. Leys goes as far as to argue that one can no longer talk of national development: 'what is no longer possible, thanks to that same global market, is development conceived of as a project for change undertaken collectively by the population of a single, medium sized country, acting through the state' (Leys, 1996, p. 41). If national development, as it has been understood, is no longer possible, an analysis of what is possible and probable becomes essential.

The second assumption of the globalization thesis is that the international system is in a process of transformation, from a relatively stable system based on US hegemony and the Cold War towards a virtual unknown. The optimistic neo-liberal assumption is that this new system, based on liberal markets, new technologies, competition and a minimal role for the state, will transform and develop the Third and former Second Worlds (Callaghy, 1993). However, globalization, as far as it can be identified, has an uneven impact upon the world. It is clear, for example, that the autonomy of the poorest states in Sub-Saharan Africa to make decisions even about development is limited. Many are caught up with questions of survival. While globalization may draw some peripheral states (the NIEs) into global industrial processes, this is not inevitable.

The benefits of globalization will exclude some states, regions and peoples. Thus if there is a globalized system, it is important to know in whose interests it operates. That is, who benefits from the emergence of a global economy? It may well be that 'the changing nature of governments, and the growth of mechanisms of collaboration, are largely a feature of the Western developed world rather than the Third World' (M. Smith, 1992, p. 261). On the other hand, it is possible to see globalization as disadvantageous to the Third World, consigning it to the role of providing cheap labour for multinational capital.

Certainly there are parts of the Third World which do not seem to be reaping many benefits. However, the increasing heterogeneity of the Third World means that there can be few such general conclusions. Instead what is needed is an examination of the precise manner in which different national or regional economies interact with a continuously changing international system. How does the international system constrain or facilitate particular policies? In many ways this is what the later dependency writers were trying to do, but they failed to appreciate the changing international system sufficiently. A more precise analysis of one group of countries, the NIEs of East Asia, and their interaction with the international system is presented in the next chapter.

Summary

This chapter has briefly charted a chronology of two major schools of development: European (orthodox) development theory and the neo-Marxist or dependency perspective, with its historical antecedent, ECLA. In particular it has sought to highlight the manner in which the different theories conceptualize and view the international system and its impact on development. While European development theory sees the obstacles to development as being internal to the developing countries, the neo-Marxists argue that the problem is structural and lies in the nature of the international system. It is clear that neither provides a complete explanation for (the lack of) development. An approach which links the national with the international is necessary.

The latter part of the chapter looked at the increasingly pervasive neo-liberal agenda and its implications in a changing global system. Contrary to the modernization-type assumptions of neo-liberalism, the system will impact differently on different states, and there are real limitations to approaches which consider the Third World to be a homogeneous problem in need of a homogeneous solution. It is to one aspect of this increasing diversity we now turn.

Part II
The Global Economy and Development

4 | The East Asian NIEs

Introduction

All Third World states were once, or still are, exporters of primary products. In Latin America, ECLA recommended the implementation of a process of ISI as a means to break the excessive dependence on primary commodity exports. Under ISI earnings from primary commodity exports, along with foreign borrowing, were used to finance the import of selected capital goods for the local manufacture of consumer goods. The large internal markets in Latin America provided a readily available demand for the locally produced manufactures. ECLA proposed ISI in the belief that there were few benefits to be had from the production of primary commodities for export. This belief, which came to be synonymous with development theory, is based on a number of assumptions.

First, and most importantly, industrialization was thought to be necessary in order to eliminate poverty and satisfy human needs. The argument is that with increases in material standards, human needs change and the demand for a wide variety of goods and more sophisticated products (such as industrial goods) increases. An economy based purely on agricultural production cannot sustain or meet the demand for industrial products, given the terms of trade (see chapter 3) for non-industrial goods.

Second, industry creates backward and forward linkages in an economy. That is, it can create an economy which is linked together in such a way that outputs from commodity production can be used as inputs for industrial production, and the industrial products can be consumed by the commodity producers. One of the main criticisms made by the plantation school (Beckford, 1972) against plantation economies was that they created disarticulated economies; that is, economies in which people consumed the things they did not produce, and produced commodities which they did not consume.

Third, industry is more technological in character than agriculture, and so is more amenable to the investment of capital. It is in the nature of capital to create more capital and hence increase wealth. This lesson was easily apparent in the industrialization of Europe when wealth increased at rates previously unheard of. For these reasons it was thought to be important that all Third World states try to industrialize.

This chapter looks at the industrialization of the East Asian NIEs, in particular at Hong Kong, Singapore, South Korea and Taiwan, whose success has been held up as invalidating the claims of the dependency theorists and attributed to the virtues of free market liberalism. We begin by briefly surveying the achievement of these states, making comparisons with other Third World states. Then we ask how it was achieved and whether the process is replicable in other Third World states. Finally we ask what lessons we can learn from the NIEs about the question of development. That is, what is their relevance for the theories of development discussed in the previous chapters? Importantly, is there a fundamental contradiction between the invasive nature of the state in the NIEs and the neo-liberal emphasis on rolling back the state?

Industrialization in the NIEs

While the necessity of industrialization is not questioned by development theories, the means by which it will be achieved often is. In Latin America the inward-looking policies of ISI were adopted from around 1935 and carried on, though modified, into the 1980s. In contrast the East Asian economies embarked upon export-oriented growth policies in the early to mid-1960s. By the 1970s the NIEs were 'an accomplished fact' while ISI was still being preached to the rest of the Third World (Mehmet, 1995).

Taiwan and South Korea had a short period of ISI from the

1940s to the 1960s, much the same as in Latin America, before changing to export-led growth. Hong Kong and Singapore, in contrast, had been outward-looking from much earlier on. This is because they are entrepôts, acting as intermediaries between primary exporting hinterlands (in this case China and Malaysia) and regional or world markets. They have no rural sectors of their own and depend on food and labour from the hinterland. They initially specialized in financial and commercial services.

In the first phase of the transition, from the 1960s to the 1970s, all four economies shifted incentives towards the export of light, labour-intensive manufactures. In the second stage, South Korea and Taiwan moved towards the manufacture of more technology- and capital-intensive sectors: automobiles, computers, electrical goods (1970 to the present). Hong Kong and Singapore, in contrast, developed large service and commercial sectors (late 1970s to the present).

The results, in terms of economic growth, have been phenomenal. Hamilton (1987) points out that never before have so many countries transformed so quickly from underdeveloped into middle-income industrial economies. Between 1970 and 1980 the average annual growth rate in Hong Kong was 9.2 per cent. Similar figures were recorded for Singapore, where the growth rate averaged 8.3 per cent, and South Korea, where the average was 9.6 per cent. During this period, the UK averaged only a 2 per cent growth rate and the USA 2.8 per cent. During the period 1980–92 high growth rates continued. The average for both Hong Kong and Singapore was 6.7 per cent, while for South Korea it was 9.4 per cent (World Bank, 1994). A comparison of growth rates in the period 1980–92 reveals the extent to which the NIEs have surpassed other groups of developing economies (see table 4.1).

Table 4.1   Regional rates of growth, 1980–92

Region	Growth (%)
Sub-Saharan Africa	−0.8
Latin America and Caribbean	−0.2
East Asian NIEs	6.2

Source: World Bank, 1994.

Is the process replicable?

One of the more frequently asked questions about the East Asian NIEs is: can the model be generalized? Can all Third World states hope one day to become like the East Asian NIEs, or are there circumstances peculiar to the individual states which do not hold for other countries or regions, such as Africa?

The question of replicability is not easily answered. One must ask what conditions and policies, internal and external, facilitated these high rates of growth, and whether they are applicable to other countries trying to industrialize. Does the international context within which these states industrialized provide the same conditions today, or has it changed so significantly that the conditions which facilitated export-led growth in the 1960s and 1970s no longer exist? In the domestic context, what cultural, economic and political conditions and policies facilitated growth? It should be apparent that even if the international system remained constant (which it has not), domestic specificities almost certainly prohibit any generalizations. However, that does not mean that there are no lessons to be learned.

The international context

ECLA and the dependency writers argued that the international system, which was capitalist in nature, was composed of core states and peripheral states. The periphery was in a less advantageous position than the core; however, this situation was not inevitable. While Frank (1969) argued that the solution was to delink, and ECLA for ISI, the East Asian economies have, in contrast to these theories, increased their links with the international system through export-led policies.

Haggard (1990) argues that international shocks and pressures, and the consequent domestic crises, have been the most powerful stimuli for changes in policy. In South Korea and Taiwan, war and reconstruction depleted finances and led to a balance of payments crisis; they were importing more than they were exporting. This provided the impetus to begin a short period of ISI. In Hong Kong the Chinese Revolution, and in Singapore the break with Malaysia, provided the impetus for

changes in economic policy. Without support from the hinterland it became essential for both Hong Kong and Singapore to
become more economically independent. As they were small
and had few domestic resources, they needed to generate non-
traditional exports. Both engaged direct foreign investment
(DFI) to finance the transition from entrepôt to export-led growth
(Haggard, 1990). In comparison while larger Latin American
states responded to external events (the 1930s world depression) by trying to shield themselves internally, the smaller East
Asian states, with fewer natural resources, were forced out into
exporting.

It is often argued that the NIEs were able to take advantage of
favourable conditions in the international economy. For example, in the 1970s, after the OPEC oil shocks there was a massive
transfer of capital to the Third World. This was due in part to
slow growth in the Northern economies. The owners of capital
went in search of new investment opportunities. Many TNCs
were attracted by cheap labour in the South and established
branches in those Third World states which were hospitable to
their presence. The high levels of infrastructure provided in
South Korea and Taiwan (part of the heritage of Japanese
occupation) made it easier to attract foreign investment.[1]

The USA was also a source of capital which played a role in the
process of industrialization in the NIEs, in particular in South
Korea. Anxious to keep South Korea friendly and to undermine
the communist regime in North Korea, the USA provided
military and economic aid in the 1960s to South Korea. Indeed
the threat of withdrawal of this aid was one factor which
stimulated the change from ISI to export-led industrialization.

One can argue that the current international system is less
hospitable to industrialization in the rest of the Third World.
The existence of more liberal (and global) markets means that
there is more competition for markets. Those producers able to
take advantage of current market conditions will be most successful. Efficiency in industry is a product of both price and also,
increasingly, technology. While the development of new technologies should make it easier to set up factories and introduce
new production processes, technology is increasingly controlled by new laws against its reproduction. This means that it
cannot simply be copied and adapted without the permission of
the owners and the payment of royalties. The Uruguay Round

of GATT negotiations (1986–94) reaffirmed and strengthened this principle. It is also still the case that most technology is produced in the North. There are thus limitations, in terms of cost and access to technology, to the type of industry which can be developed.

Another argument is that while export-oriented industrialization may work for a small group of states, if all the Third World were exporting manufactures, there would either be increased protectionism from the North and/or a limited demand for the exports of any one country. However, evidence suggests that the market for industrial exports of the East Asian NIEs expanded, despite high levels of protectionism in the 1980s. This is due, it is claimed, to the ability of the NIEs to manoeuvre around protectionist barriers. For example, in the 1970s protectionism against labour-intensive industries such as textiles increased. In addition, new technologies threatened the NIEs advantage in labour. The NIEs thus upgraded their industries and diversified into new lines. Hong Kong decided to allow the share of industry in GNP to fall and placed more emphasis on expanding its service sector. Moreover, all the NIEs sought out new trading partners in the Third World and the socialist bloc.

Protectionism has thus forced the NIEs to upgrade their products and diversify their product base. In the 1990s, with trade supposedly becoming more liberal, protectionism may have declined; for example, the Multifibre Agreement (MFA) will be phased out by the World Trade Organization (WTO), established in 1995.[2] However, new types of protectionism, reworded in the language of common markets, labour and environmental standards, are likely to increase, making it difficult for other Third World states to follow the NIEs. Nevertheless, a new tier of rapidly industrializing economies has been identified in Malaysia, Thailand and China as well as Chile.

The domestic context

Although the international system creates the context within which states act, they do not respond uniformly to it; thus the national development process varies from state to state. It would be impossible to set out the precise details of the domestic context of the industrialization process in all four NIEs here. Instead I will briefly list some of the factors which have facilitated the transition to successful, export-led industrialization. What becomes apparent is that the extent to which any set of variables can be said to be responsible, and therefore provide a model, is very limited. It is clear that there has been a set of shifting variables.

Haggard (1990) seeks to answer the question of why similarly situated states pursue different policies. In reference to the NIEs of Latin America and those of East Asia, he asks why the former pursued ISI for such a long period and the latter quickly moved on to export-oriented industrialization strategies. He argues that the relationship between economic growth and political institutions (the nature of decision-making structures and the policy instruments available) is the key. Thus when looking at the domestic context, it is not just the specific economic policies which are important, but also the political. To this I would add the specific cultural context, which also determines the nature of the response to specific situations, as well as the state's room for manoeuvre. There are nevertheless a few general statements which can be made about the NIEs.

Initially the proponents of liberalism held up the East Asian NIEs as examples of the success of free markets, in direct contrast to the lack of economic success in Africa and other parts of Asia where the state had pursued an interventionist policy. More recently it has become apparent that industrialization was very much a state-directed project. Even the World Bank has now accepted that the NIE experience demonstrated 'the necessity for forceful, systematic, and sustained economic intervention by a strong centralised state pursuing a coherent long term development strategy' (Leys, 1996, p. 49). This is a key point to note. The precise nature of the intervention will be explored further on.

It is also important to stress the authoritarian nature of government during the process. While the East Asian NIEs have been more outward-oriented than other states, for example in Latin America, they have not necessarily been more liberal. While some of the NIEs are moving towards democratic government, it is as yet a slow and limited process (Gills and Rocamora, 1992). The peculiar mix of managed capitalism and authoritarian regime is unlikely to be advocated in an era when development has been replaced by a new buzz word: democracy.

We should note too that the policies pursued embodied certain endogenous cultural values, such as the importance of the family and the community (Mehmet, 1995). This fact has given rise to explanations stressing the Confucian work ethic: 'Confucianism – formerly considered to be the cause of China's backwardness – has become in recent years the explanation for its economic take-off as well as for the Japanese and Korean miracles' (S. Amin, 1988, pp. 60–1). Its work ethic involves obedience to hierarchy, leading to devotion to the family and service to the state characteristic of the NIEs, China and Japan. On their own these are insufficient, but the specific cultural characteristics of the region must form part of the explanation for the process. Indeed these factors are important because they point towards a distinct, non-European process. For example, the emergence of regions of mixed rural (rice-growing) and non-rural activity surrounding large urban centres – for example in Hong Kong – points towards a particular mix of culture and ecology and emphasizes the way in which local conditions interact with national and international processes. Or it could be argued that the strong value placed on education facilitated the creation of a highly skilled and flexible labour force. The emphasis on discipline and respect for authority that was part of that education meant that the state and its agents could play a more directly interventionist role in people's lives.

Culture has nevertheless often been excluded from development theory, perhaps because it is difficult to quantify and, more importantly, to identify. It is not often clear, for example, what 'the national' culture is where more than one ethnic group exists (Hettne, 1993). In Hong Kong there is now a division between those who consider themselves part of China, and those who do not.

How has the state acted as an economic catalyst in the industrialization process? One mechanism was to set up incentives to specific types of production at different stages. It was possible for South Korea and Taiwan to move towards the production of more capital-intensive processes in the 1970s because the state gave fiscal and financial incentives to do so. This type of intervention, called *industrial targeting*, helped the development of the business classes in South Korea, and enabled the state to mobilize capital and target it into highly productive areas. Industrial targeting was practised less in Hong Kong because it had the benefit of an existing commercial establishment, inherited from China.

In order to make their exports more competitive, the NIEs introduced exchange rate devaluations. At the same time, selective import liberalization made importing key inputs easy and the import of all else difficult, thereby ensuring there was no major BOP deficit. By keeping external debt to a minimum, reinvestment and development of new industries were possible. These were also facilitated by encouraging high rates of savings among the populace, which could then be used for investment purposes.

The success of industrialization in East Asia can also be linked to weak labour interests. The state has been able to control the labour market by banning unions, for example in South Korea after a number of strikes.[3] This keeps wages low and creates an atmosphere of imposed loyalty to the company, so that labour is prepared to work longer hours.

At the same time, the Japanese principle of innovative imitation – that is, copying while improving the product – demands a highly skilled labour force. Incentives were thus given by the state to train unskilled and semi-skilled labour, so that by the time the transition to high-technology production was made there was already a well-educated and trained labour force.

Often as industrialization occurs income inequality increases. However, in Taiwan and South Korea rapid growth was accompanied by an improved income distribution. This can be explained by the restructuring of property rights through land redistribution and by demography (there were low rates of population growth) as well as by deliberate redistributive policies.

In Taiwan and South Korea there were massive land reforms after Japanese colonialism. These were designed to increase food production, and left a relatively egalitarian distribution of land and income prior to the 1960s. This has meant less dissatisfaction among the agricultural classes. In addition, many parts of the agricultural sector have been modernized and integrated with the industrial/commercial sector.

In South Korea the initial levelling of incomes changed with the transition to high technology industrialization in the 1970s. This worsening of income distribution has been attributed to the

increased concentration of capital in the hands of large industrial families. Nevertheless, the stress on growth with equity
remains an important part of the development process.

Hawthorn (1991) argues that what distinguishes the Third
World from the First World is not so much the preoccupation
with national income (all states are concerned about this to one
degree or another) as the fact that the Third World, diverse as it
is, has tended to use public power and authority to develop
commerce, trade, industry and the correct financial conditions to
facilitate development. Thus the state is a crucial player in providing the right conditions for economic development. What distinguishes different Third World states is the relative success or
failure of the state in pursuing its ends. Unfortunately this maxim
provides little help for those who tend to fail (Hettne, 1995a).

The East Asian NIEs were clearly successful in achieving their
objectives in the period under review. A particular domestic
configuration of forces – a strong and authoritarian developmental state, industrial targeting, land and income redistribution, weak labour interests, a well-trained labour force, the
ability to adjust production and adapt technology, and a high
savings rate – all played a part in a unique process which was
able to take advantage of a favourable international climate.

The NIEs and development theory

One explanation for the success of the NIEs is that they concentrated on those products in which they had a comparative
advantage at the time. When they lost this in simple manufactures, they moved on to more capital-intensive, higher-technol-
ogy products or into the service sector. This is the liberal
explanation which holds up the NIEs to the rest of the Third
World as market miracles.

A. G. Frank (1981) argues that there was a general economic
crisis in the 1970s which shifted the international division of
labour, so that industrial processes became located in the Third
World, which offered the advantage of cheap labour. There is,
he claims, little qualitative difference between this model and
the traditional one based by the export of raw materials. Thus
the NIEs became cheap labour for the core states, providing
access to cheaper industrial products and raising the material

quality of life in the North. By this account the dependency model of underdevelopment is perpetuated.

It is equally possible to view the NIEs as what Cardoso and Faletto (see chapter 3) would call *dependent development*; that is, development conditioned by the structural position of the NIEs in the world economy. The benefit of this analysis is that it recognizes a distinction between different types of industrialization in the First and Third Worlds. However, this does not do justice to the achievements of the NIEs, which are not simply in terms of economic growth.

The NIEs also embody aspects peculiar to the region (rather than to all the Third World) such as a socially cohesive, non-Western cultural value system which was harnessed by the state. Economic development also depends on political stability. There is a correlation between successful industrialization and the avoidance of the uneven effects of development (Hirst and Thompson, 1996). The state in the NIEs played a key role in ensuring an educated and flexible labour force able to move from sector to sector as necessary. This lessened the extent to which people felt left out of the process. Thus the explanation for the NIE success also lies in the (wider) range of possible options open to non-democratic states.

Authoritarian developmentalism in East Asia did involve a 'human face': the state used its control of political power to promote public investment in education, housing, infrastructure and reducing fertility rates. Thus the state did perceive the need to translate growth into specific social policies which did not exclude particular sectors of society and so the benefits of industrialization were spread. The rest of this section looks briefly at the impact of policies on education and welfare, and on female employment.[4]

Education and welfare

One way to measure the well-being of a population is by the Physical Quality of Life Index (PQLI). This combines infant mortality, life expectancy and literacy. The possible score lies between zero and one hundred. By this index the NIEs steadily increased their scores and were on par with many First World countries by the 1970s (see table 4.2).

Table 4.2   PQLI for selected years

Period	Korea	Taiwan	Singapore	Hong Kong
Prior to 1960	58	63	n.a.	n.a.
1970	76	87	83	86
1980	85	88	86	92
1985	88	94	91	95

Source: Haggard, 1990.

An alternative measurement is the UN Human Development Index (HDI), which combines life expectancy, literacy and purchasing power. The range of possible scores is from zero to one. On this scale in 1987, South Korea scored 0.903, Singapore 0.899, and Hong Kong 0.936. Again, these are fairly high scores for countries considered part of the Third World. (See chapter 6 for more discussion of the HDI.)

On both indicators the NIEs are doing fairly well in terms of human well-being. However, South Korea and Taiwan started quite high on the scales. Even before the transition to export-led growth in the 1960s, there was heavy emphasis on education. This of course tempers the conclusion that industrial growth has increased the quality of life significantly. By the time of the transition, they had a relatively well-educated labour force. In 1960, Korea had 94 per cent of primary school children enrolled, while in Singapore the corresponding figure is 112 per cent.[5] High levels of enrolment have continued in primary, secondary and tertiary education, exceeding the norm for countries with similar levels of GNP.

Where the process of export-led growth has been copied elsewhere in Asia, it is difficult to find similar indicators. In Malaysia the literacy rate was 60 per cent in 1980. Primary and secondary school enrolment was 102 per cent and 56 per cent respectively in 1987 (Tan, 1993). While these levels are not as high as the NIEs', they are above the Third World average. However, part of Malaysia's and Thailand's success is based on the provision of cheap labour, with a shortage of skilled labour preventing the transition to more high-technology industries.

Female employment

One of the most striking aspects of industrialization in East Asia has been the increase in female employment (see tables 4.3 and 4.4). This contradicts previous ideas that the process would push women out of employment (Boserup, 1970).

Table 4.3 Percentage share of women in non-agricultural employment, 1975–87

Country	1975	1985	1987
Korea	33	38	39
Singapore	30	36	38

This includes employment in industry as well as in service sectors.
Average in Africa 1972–82: 24.3 per cent, and in Latin America and the Caribbean 1970–81: 35.3 per cent.
Source: Standing, 1992.

While the increase in female employment may seem positive at first sight, it is important to look not just at the numbers employed but also at the conditions of female employment. On the one hand, a job provides women with extra income and a degree of independence and consequent security. However, increases in female employment are often closely allied to the erosion of labour regulations, so that if wages are low and job security is limited, the absolute benefit of increased female employment is questionable.

Table 4.4 Percentage of women in manufacturing, 1975–85

Country	1975	1980	1985
Hong Kong	52	50	50
Korea	n.a.	45	42
Singapore	41	47	48

Source: Standing, 1992.

Women in the NIEs have been employed mainly in the lighter industries, such as textiles, and they are not usually employed at managerial level. Women also tend to receive lower wages for the same work (see table 4.5). Indeed they are often employed because they do not agitate for higher wages.[6]

Table 4.5 Female earnings as a percentage of male earnings in manufacturing, 1980–7

Country	1980	1985	1987
Korea	45	47	50
Hong Kong	78	79	76
Singapore	62	63	58

Source: Standing, 1992.

There are also issues of leave entitlement, benefits, and maternity leave, which are often not regulated. In 1988 none of the NIEs had ratified the International Labour Organization (ILO) Convention which stipulates the principle of equal pay for equal work. The argument is that if maternity leave, for example, was made compulsory and the employers had to pay, this would discourage female employment.

In conclusion, while the number of women employed in the East Asian NIEs is actually higher than in some of the more recent converts to export-led industrialization, such as Mauritius or the Philippines, the conditions of employment remain poor. Improvements will be slow where unions are forbidden and labour is controlled by authoritarian governments.

Summary

There are a number of lessons which can be learnt from the NIEs. First, contrary to the theories of development we discussed in the last chapter, it is clear that the international system is not the only factor responsible for the success or failure of development policies. While none of the theories examined would deny a role for the domestic context, they did not examine sufficiently the interplay of domestic and international factors. It is in the unique combination of internal and external constraints and opportunities that a more satisfactory explanation may be found.

Second, a specific mix of policies was adopted in relation to the particular circumstances of the NIEs. The NIEs do not simply demonstrate the success of liberal markets. They are instead a pragmatic but culturally particular response to world market conditions. These circumstances are not necessarily replicable in other states. While this may seem like common sense, it has not always been accepted. Nevertheless, the fact of the specificity of industrialization in East Asia does not mean that the NIEs are the lucky exceptions, unlikely to be repeated. It merely means that we should not attempt to generalize from this experience. Development is not a formal model, but an on-going discourse, aware of its temporal and spatial context.

Third, in terms of education and employment policies, there is no necessary correlation between growth and other dimensions of development. While growth creates the capacity to meet more needs, this requires specific intervention. The ability of the state in the NIEs to implement growth with redistribution policies and to target education is in part due to its authoritarian status. The fact that the prosperity of the population has increased has helped to maintain the legitimacy of the state. However, as the state becomes more responsive to the demands of an electorate, its room for manoeuvre will decrease, rather than increase.

5 | The Environment and Development

Introduction

There is now sufficient scientific evidence to suggest that the environment cannot sustain current patterns of industrial development indefinitely. This necessarily has implications for the manner in which we think about development. Traditional development theories have tended to assume the necessity of industrialization, but this is now being questioned by approaches which seek to find alternative or counterpoint solutions (Hettne, 1995a). In this chapter the focus is on ecological aspects of 'another' development, and its manifestation in *sustainable development*, as a new and contested paradigm of both IR and development.

The environmental crisis adds a new dimension to North–South relations, for it is in the sphere of the environment that the North has become persuaded of the significance of the South's development policies and prospects. The link between the environment and development has thus become one of international political significance. The purpose of this chapter is to demonstrate that the environment is intricately linked to development, but that the parameters of the equation are not always clear. This fact is most obvious in the concept of sustainable development.

The chapter begins with an examination of the rise of environmental issues on the international agenda, leading up to the Bruntland Report and the UN Conference on the Environment and Development (UNCED) in 1992. The second section looks at different approaches to environmental issues. The final section examines the concept of sustainable development and what its realization might mean for the question of development. An alternative development based on the needs of particular regions – eco-development – offers both a sustainable and endogenous approach, and a critique of the preceding 'global' ones.

The environment and international relations

The environment can be construed as the physical context in which we live, encompassing the atmosphere (air, ozone layer), the lithosphere or geosphere (mineral deposits, soil, rocks), the hydrosphere[1] (deep sea bed, rivers, glaciers) and the biosphere (vegetation, habitation, all living organisms). All four sectors are closely related and together they make up the *ecosphere*, the study of which is known as *ecology*.

The physical environment is regarded by economists as an open system. This means that, in order to function, the economy takes certain things from the environment (raw materials, fuel) and puts back certain things (waste materials, carbon dioxide). Over a long period it is essential to balance what is taken out and what is put back in, because it takes considerable time for the environment to adjust to new patterns of resource use. If the balance is not maintained, *environmental degradation* will occur. This can be defined as 'the breaching or rupture of ecosystemic toleration in a systematic and reiterated fashion' (Saurin, 1994, p. 47).

Importantly, humanity lives within the environment. We cannot survive without the support of the ecosphere, although the reverse is not true. Over the past few decades there has been an increasing awareness of this fact. Although the scientific community has long recognized and studied the relationship between humans and the environment, and non-governmental organizations (NGOs), Green political parties and social movements have raised public awareness about the integral nature of the environment, its study by social scientists (except anthropologists) is a relatively new phenomenon.

The link between the environment and IR is not remarkable. Geopolitics is one area of the discipline which has looked closely at the resources of a given state, or group of states, in the determination of foreign policy. Also, the study of imperialism is closely connected to the distribution of resources throughout the world. To this end the environment has been a means for foreign policy goals. Nevertheless, the growth in environmental awareness, marked by the increased discussion of environmental issues in global rather than national or regional arenas, has only come about in the past two decades.

Part of the reason for this is a growing awareness of ecological interdependence. The environment, and the consequences of its misuse, are shared by all states. It is no longer possible for politicians to ignore this; those who make decisions increasingly have to take account of their environmental implications. Also, the end of the Cold War (see chapter 8) has meant that less energy is being devoted to ideological battles, and this in turn has meant that the warnings issued by scientists many years ago about the global nature of the problem can now be heeded.

The environment is not, however, simply a physical context. It can also be considered as a social construction (Redclift, 1987, p. 3). That is, not only are there different physical environments, but the environment means different things to, and is transformed by, those who use it. For example, the environment played a particular role in the industrial development of Western Europe. In the nineteenth century the environment came to be seen as separate from the social world: a natural world which could be harnessed and used to increase productive capacities. Human abilities, through rationality, were deemed superior to nature. There was little appreciation of the natural limits of the environment, or of its interrelationship with human progress. Indeed the achievement of economic growth was seen to be possible only through the exploitation of natural resources.

In 1972 this widely held assumption was challenged by a Malthusian-inspired *absolute limits to growth* perspective.[2] The Club of Rome report, *The Limits to Growth* (Meadows et al., 1972), brought to public attention the environmental constraints on development. The report argued that if current growth trends (in population, industrialization and pollution) continued unchanged, the limits to growth would be reached sometime in the next hundred years.[3] The pessimistic conclusions of the report challenged the assumption that continued economic growth was desirable, and opened the Pandora's box that is the question of the environment and development.

From the 1970s, the UN, the scientific community and public concern for the environment grew, partly as a result of a series of environmental disasters (Chernobyl, Bhopal) but also as more scientific evidence emerged. In 1972 the Stockholm Conference (the UN Conference on the Human Environment) brought together delegates from over one hundred states, plus UN and intergovernmental organizations. In so doing it lent legitimacy to the place of environmental concerns in international relations (Thomas, 1992). Stockholm also created the UN Environmental Programme (UNEP).

It was at Stockholm that divisions between the North and the South on the environment were first made apparent. Whereas the North wanted to focus on issues of population, control of resources and limits to growth, the South wanted attention to issues which affected their everyday lives such as shelter, food and clean drinking water (Miller, 1995). There was an emerging tension between the basic needs of the South and the Northern desire to protect the environment in a particular manner. This tension continued into the 1980s. On the one hand, scientific research focused on ozone depletion and climate change; on the other hand, the lost development decade (see chapter 4) left many Third World states in an economically worse situation than they had been in at the beginning of the decade.

In 1987 the World Commission on the Environment and Development (WCED) published its now famous report, *Our Common Future*, which put the concept of sustainable development on the international agenda. The Bruntland Report (as it became known, after the chair of the commission) argued that a new era of growth was necessary: one which could simultaneously meet the needs of the poor and preserve the environment for future generations.

In this context the UN called for a major conference on the environment and development (UNCED), which was held in 1992. The Earth Summit in Brazil was certainly the largest environmental conference to date, with representatives from over 170 states and thousands of NGOs and TNCs. However, once again divisions were apparent, although this time the diversity of interests within the South, as well as the North, was evident.

For example, climate change is caused largely by past and current industrial activity, which has mainly taken place in the

North.[4] However, the effects of climate change will be felt not just in the polar regions: small islands are particularly vulnerable to rises in sea levels, as is agricultural production to changes in weather conditions. It is thus likely to affect most immediately the livelihood of those Southern states (small island ones above all) which rely heavily on agriculture as a source of income.

At Rio some Northern states, especially the USA, were not willing to alter their industrial consumption significantly. On the other hand, the Scandinavian states and the European Union (EU) were in favour of cutbacks (though modest ones) in greenhouse emissions. In the South some industrializing states were reluctant to cut back on their industrial development and felt that the onus of responsibility lay with the polluters: the North. They also recognized the cost of changes in technology which would have to be met by the North.

What emerged from Rio was a treaty which recognized that the North would have to make more cutbacks than the South, and even that the North would have to meet the agreed costs of mitigating climate change in the South. However, the treaty has been seen as inadequate in the rate of cutbacks; that is, it will not make any significant impact on the rate of global warming. Also the South was unable to persuade the North actually to commit itself to any significant financial and technological transfers (Paterson, 1994, p. 176).

The environment has provided a new context and focus for IR. Recognizing the interdependence inherent in the scarcity of resources, it is imperative that solutions be found to meet the needs of both the North and the South. If the fact of major environmental degradation can be demonstrated, the question which arises is: who is responsible for taking the appropriate action? Is it those who are historically responsible for the damage, or all members of the international community? And this refers not only to states but also to the many TNCs whose production sites are located throughout the world. Furthermore, who will pay for the protection of the environment, and where will the funds come from? These questions were only partly dealt with at Rio.

In addition, as Thomas points out, 'at the most fundamental level the causes of environmental degradation have not been addressed, and without this efforts to tackle the crisis are bound to fail' (Thomas, 1994, p. 2). The causes lie not so much in the specific practices of a given state, as in the (liberal) ideology which holds to the necessity and desirability of growth, industrialization, increased consumption and competitiveness. It is thus at one and the same time caused by the ideology of development and by the logic of globalization.

It is clear that there was no single approach to the environment at Rio, even if there was a dominant one. In the following section we identify three main approaches to the environment and development: the *conventional*, the *biocentric* and the *sustainability*. Within these three approaches exist many diverse views, some of which cut across the divisions. They are therefore presented as ideal types rather than monolithic categories, designed to show that the question of the environment, its crucial relationship to development, and its centrality in IR is a contested one.[5]

Approaches

The conventional approach

The conventional approach is underpinned by an *anthropocentric* belief system, which holds that human beings are the centre of the universe, and/or that the non-human world is a means to human ends (Dobson, 1990, p. 63). While the first may be an essential element of being human (O'Riordan, 1981), and recognizes the central role that humans do play in the environment, the latter is more instrumental in its calculations. The emergence of this latter attitude coincides with the rise of industrialization, when increased material consumption based on the conquest of nature became accepted as both possible and desirable. The drive to industrialization, initially in Europe, was later exported to the Third World through theories of modernization, which argued that all societies could become industrial if the right preconditions were created. Thus the conventional approach is allied to European development theory.

In terms of solutions, the conventional approach is reformist, arguing that the environmental crisis can be dealt with by the extant international system if a few small changes are made. Because environmental problems do not respect state boundaries, it is important to find the means to get states to cooperate in finding and implementing global solutions. As this perspective operates essentially within an anthropocentric belief system, the solutions provided are designed to allow for the continued welfare of people. Thus the question which is asked is not how the environment can be preserved for its own sake, but how it can be preserved for the continued use of humans.

Most environmental problems are viewed as scientifically solvable equations. That is, it is assumed there can be an objective solution to problems which are seen as essentially technical in nature; such as fitting catalytic converters to cars, rather than asking why we need cars, or banning the import of woods from tropical forests, instead of asking about the nature of international trade. The concerns of this perspective are about order, rather than change. The question which is asked is how states can cooperate to find solutions to environmental problems rather than how environmental problems are created (Paterson, 1994).

The biocentric approach

At the other end of the spectrum, the biocentric approach attributes intrinsic value to nature for its own sake, and does not permit its exploitation in pursuit of ever-increasing wealth. Humankind is thought to form only one part of a large whole, the biosphere. Because the biosphere is not infinite in its resources, these should be consumed with care and responsibility, in terms of needs rather than wants. A biocentric belief system thus highlights the interrelationship and interdependence of the plant and animal species and the planet.[6]

As such it challenges the views of the Enlightenment, which sees humans as superior to the rest of the universe. The biocentric approach argues that caring for the environment requires a radical change in our relationship with it. It is not enough merely to manage the environment; instead the underlying assumptions of the social and political organization of society need to be questioned. Thus in terms of solutions, this perspective argues that the current international system cannot deal with the environmental crisis, and consequently it is the system which is in need of radical changes.

The sustainability approach

The third approach considered here is that of sustainability. This charts a middle road between the conventional 'development equals unlimited growth' perspective, and the biocentric 'hostility towards growth because it threatens the ecological balance' perspective (Hettne, 1995a, p. 190).

The concept of sustainability was made popular by the Bruntland Report (WCED, 1987), which explicitly linked the question of the environment to that of development. Sustainable development, WCED argued, involves improving people's material resources at a rate which can be maintained for an indefinite period. The three main components of a sustainable approach are:

- intergenerational equity – allowing future generations the possibility of development;
- ecosystem interdependence – recognizing the symbiotic relationship between humanity and the environment;
- human development – providing people with the opportunity to meet their basic needs (K. Brown et al., 1993).

Nevertheless, the debate on sustainability is less clear cut than it at first appears. On the one hand, sustainability appears to recognize that the conventional approach to development, which sees industrialization as progress, has led to environmental degradation. On the other hand, the report calls for a new era of growth. The South has accused the North of eco-imperialism in trying to constrain its development prospects, and described the report as representing 'yet another attempt . . . to reassert and rationalise Northern global ideological hegemony' (Graf, 1992, p. 553). This debate will be elaborated in the following section.

Sustainable development, 'another' development?

One of the most challenging statements that has arisen from environmental debate is the need to link development and the environment through the concept of sustainable development.

WCED was set up by the UN in 1983 as an independent commission specifically to address the relationship between the environment and development. Its report, published in 1987, followed two previous UN commissions, the Brandt and the Palme Commissions, which had produced *North–South: A Programme for Survival* (1980) and *Common Security* (1982) respectively. All three commissions perceived an impending, if not extant, global or common crisis.

Our Common Future (WCED, 1987) pointed out that the environment does not exist in isolation from human actions and concerns, and that development cannot be viewed as something which poor states do to become rich. Rather 'the environment is where we all live, and development is what we all do' (WCED, 1987, p. xi). Furthermore, 'there has been a growing realization in national governments and multilateral institutions that it is impossible to separate economic development issues from environmental issues ... many forms of development erode the environmental resources upon which they must be based, and environmental degradation can undermine economic development' (WCED, 1987, p. 3).

The Bruntland Commission used the catch-phrase 'sustainable development', which it defined as 'development which seeks to meet the needs and aspirations of the present without compromising the ability to meet those of the future' (WCED, 1987, p. 40), to try to unite as many different states, interests and perspectives as possible. It therefore seems inevitable that the idea is vague and open to many different interpretations. Consequently the utility of the concept has been widely questioned. Richardson (1994) claims that it is a political fudge: a convenient form of words, sufficiently vague to allow conflicting interests to uphold it. Others have argued that it seeks to depoliticize development, and its crucial relationship to the international system, by focusing on an issue which everyone thinks is now important, the environment (Graf, 1992). Sustainable development has thus become a catch-phrase that all governments and international organizations subscribe to, but the practice of which is questionable.

Another problem surrounds the need for governments to provide economic benefits and at the same time to protect the environment. 'There is an understandable and unavoidable tension everywhere between the demands for employment, improved wages, and living conditions today and the environmental sustainability of the economic policies implemented to achieve these objectives' (Pantin, 1994, p. 10). The question is therefore how to reconcile economic development and sustainability. That is, how does one achieve *sustainable* development? This demands in the first instance a clearer understanding of the concept and the contradictions contained within it.

Indeed, is it possible to salvage something meaningful from this concept? This would require first the recognition of the failure of most development models to date; that is, the failure of theories of modernization, and of dependency, as well as the failure of fifty years of development assistance by the UN to deal adequately with world poverty, or to take the environment into account in the drive to modernize.

'Another' development questions actually existing development, and seeks to find alternative or counterpoint solutions. It is usually associated with small-scale solutions, ecological concerns, popular participation, grass-roots democracy and the reinforcement of community (Hettne, 1995a). Its origins lie in the 1970s, and are evident in the campaign for a NIEO, and in support for basic needs approaches (BNAs) and ideas of self-reliance. The focus is on the content rather than the form of development. Thus growth in GNP may facilitate development, but it is important to ask whether it does. On the other hand, it may be possible to have development without an increase in GNP if existing resources are used differently.

The main components of 'another' development are reproduced in Hettne (1995a). They are:

- need-oriented – concerned with meeting people's material and non-material needs;
- endogenous – solutions must emerge from each society, rather than be imposed;
- self-reliant – each society relies primarily on its own strength and resources;
- ecologically sound – paying attention to the limits of local ecosystems and global resources;
- based on structural transformation – enabling participation and self-management of local, regional and global communities.

It is clear that existing development falls short of these ideals. Nevertheless, 'another' development is an appeal to development which is not yet, to the way development ought to be structured. As such it is a normative approach, which has arisen out of the obvious contradictions and shortfalls of actual development. With this in mind we can examine the components of a more credible sustainable development.

If there is no single definition of development, except perhaps one which is too general to be meaningful, the concept of sustainable development, like many other developments before it, suggests the question: what type of development is sustainable? If it is to be differentiated from previous development models, it seems to require a break from the drive to industrialize. Alternatively (and this seems to be the most widely accepted idea, certainly within the conventional approach), it could mean continuing the drive towards industrialization in the Third World, but restricting it to that based on environmental regeneration. Industrial growth could then be espoused if it took place along a different route.

Yet development equated with growth has long been challenged within development studies. The BNA, which arose in the 1970s, recognized that economic growth did not necessarily eliminate poverty, improve welfare or meet basic needs; a key part of the definition of sustainable development.

Important to this debate is the distinction between needs and wants; that is, between what is necessary or unnecessary for the living of a meaningful life. Some authors have included the word 'basic' before 'needs' in an attempt to be more explicit about the distinction between basic needs and non-basic wants. They point out that it is easy for the rich to argue that some of their taken-for-granted commodities are needs rather than wants, while it seems obvious that the basic needs of a large percentage of the world's population are not being met.

Yet there has been no consensus on a single way to determine basic needs. If universal and objective standards are chosen to measure basic needs in different parts of the world, it is important to ask whose standards are chosen. Indeed, can needs be quantified and measured in this manner? As the lowest common denominator, it seems possible to argue that adequate food, water, shelter and clothing constitute the basic material needs. Above this we can say very little. When non-material needs are considered as well, the definition becomes more difficult.

Alternatively, it is possible to see needs as historically and culturally particular. Thus differently situated people require different amounts of goods to satisfy the same needs (A. Sen, 1992). The adequacy of food, water, shelter and clothing will be different for different people. Is it possible to argue in favour of basic needs, while being sensitive to different cultural traditions and different social conditions (Seabright, 1993, p. 407)? This would involve recognizing the universal nature of basic needs, while acknowledging diversity of need, even within the South.

The question of development constantly throws forth the question of whether we should look at local traditions or whether it is possible to identify some universal account of what constitutes development, and to assess these traditions in the light of it (Nussbaum and Sen, 1993, p. 4). If the former is chosen, it is possible to respect different approaches to development, but it may cover up gross injustices or inequalities. On the other hand, our search for a universal account of development may protect those who are oppressed by particular systems, but we have no adequate way of identifying the origins and list of suitable norms.

Sustainable development also embodies the notion that the needs of present and future generations should be met. That is, we have obligations to meet the needs of the existing poor – intragenerational equity – and not to meet the needs of present generations at the expense of future ones – intergenerational equity. Yet how does one protect the future of as yet unborn generations if the needs of present ones are not being met?

The problem of the survival of people and their livelihoods in the South, and the differentiated standards of living between regions and countries has not been adequately addressed by the sustainability debate (Pantin, 1994). Most countries in the North have the resources to meet the basic needs of most of the population; at the same time, the North faces significant environmental problems (high levels of toxic waste, low levels of biodiversity). In the South many people still live in conditions of poverty such that contemplating and planning for the future is a luxury. Thus 'a low initial level of environmental quality forces resource users to discount the future heavily. Poor people faced with marginal environmental conditions have no choice but to opt for immediate benefits at the expense of long run sustainability in their livelihoods' (Barbier and Markandaya, 1989, quoted in Pantin, 1994, p. 6). The solution lies in enabling the poor to meet their needs through more sustainable methods.

Yet what do we mean by 'sustainable' in this context? The authors of the Bruntland Report clearly meant 'sustainable' in terms of the environment's carrying capacity. That is, it is recognized that there are non-renewable resources (fossil fuels and minerals such as bauxite) which, when depleted, will no longer exist. In addition there are some resources which are renewable (fisheries, forests), but at a much slower rate than that of current consumption. There is also the possibility of creating new resources, but these tend to require the use of existing ones. In addition, pollution causes environmental decay. We are left with an equation whose parameters are unknown, but which tends towards saying that there are ecological limits to continued consumption and growth, and that it is perhaps wiser to conserve than to ignore potential catastrophe.

Malthus, who wrote about limits of population growth in the nineteenth century, worried about the absolute limits of the environment. He argued that while population grows exponentially or geometrically (constantly doubling itself), resources only grow arithmetically. This equation would lead to a situation whereby population would outgrow the capacity of the environment to provide for it. His contribution to the debate led to the idea of a *steady state economy*, in which growth and population would remain constant over time. He also argued for the restriction of population growth, an argument which has resurfaced time and time again.[7]

However, the Bruntland Report did not advocate a no-growth policy. Instead it argued that economic growth was still possible, if it was sustainable growth: 'we see . . . the possibility for a new era of economic growth, one that must be based on policies that sustain and expand the environment resource base' (WCED, 1987, p. 1). Furthermore, growth was essential in the Third World because poverty encouraged environmentally unsustainable practices. But while there was no rejection of growth per se, there were few specific recommendations on 'how sustainable economic growth can be recognised and distinguished from the patently unsustainable variety' (Etkins, 1992, p. 31).

The commitment of the international community to sustainability – to the need to preserve the biological systems which underpin the global economy – remains questionable. At one level the ecosystem will survive without human beings, but this threat does not urge individual states into action. If humanity did become extinct, it would affect all states equally. At this extreme it would therefore not be rational to enter into precautionary measures unless all states were doing the same thing.

Furthermore, there are many uncertainties about the rate of destruction of the environment. Governments are not usually prone to act with long-term, uncertain possibilities in mind, especially if there are short-term economic crises at hand. However, some states have seen fit to act to protect the environment, if only in specific issue areas.[8] This limited cooperation is not unprecedented, and it arises from a perceived threat to the future well-being of the environment which we all rely on. Preventive action may protect the future, even if that future is unknown.

Nevertheless, the divisions between groups of states, in particular the North and the South, as well as within those states, are still obvious. The tension between the lack of development and the need to conserve, and hence not to modernize, remains. The North still has the power and the resources to set the international environmental agenda, and has chosen to focus on those issues that affect it most directly, such as global climate change and ozone depletion.

The South, on the other hand, has had less success in forging any global consensus on the problem of development, except inasmuch as development practice is seen to threaten the global environment. But the South can bargain on climate change, because the North needs its cooperation in order to deal with the problem. Rational national interest alone should cause the North to shoulder the financial costs of global climate change, because it has the most to lose (in terms of lifestyle options, industrial output) if that is not dealt with. It is in the South's interest to establish firmly a more explicit link between the environment and development.

In terms of solutions, it may be that at the international level the parameters can be set, but the nature of the constituent units means that, like development models, environmental solutions cannot be imposed from outside. There is no universal consensus and no means of enforcement. Agreements must be entered into voluntarily. Many issues, such as shared river pollution, require regional or local solutions rather than global ones (even if they are a by-product of a larger international system). Thus *eco-development* models (discussed below), with their focus on local communities, have something to offer which is more in keeping with the idea of 'another' development.

Sustainable development, as presented by the Bruntland Commission and reinforced in UNCED, can be seen as an attempt to bridge two distinct positions: the tradition of continued growth and development, and the natural limits to growth which is inherently part of nature. It was not an attempt to rethink the relationship between the North and the South in the international system, and it did not recognize the failure of most development models to date to provide for the basic needs of substantial numbers of people. As such it assumed a consensus around the conventional approach which does not exist, as was made apparent by the minimal achievements at Rio.

Eco-development

There are, as mentioned, other approaches to the relationship between the environment and development, many of which originate in the Third World and constitute attempts to forge 'another' development. Eco-development, for example, puts forward an alternative to perspectives which focus on the global:

> Eco development is a style of development that, in each eco region, calls for specific solutions to the particular problems of the region in the light of cultural as well as ecological data and long term as well as immediate needs. Accordingly it operates with criteria of progress that are related to each particular case, and adaptation to the environment plays an important role. (I. Sachs, 1974, p. 9)

Eco-development thus views the environment and development as a means towards an end. The argument is that in the South, the primary concern is survival before sustainability.

Thus the environment cannot be an end until basic needs are met. However, survival should not be at the expense of the environment, because in the long run this is unsustainable for humans as well. Indeed economic growth is not as important as improving the situation of a particular eco-region.

Eco-development would require at the very least a radical restructuring of the concept of development. It is concerned with self-reliance, in terms not of autarchy, but of the historical and relative needs of each eco-region: being able to optimize the balance between population, local resources and culturally determined lifestyle (Riddell, 1981, p. 5). There are thus no models to emulate; the future lies in the ecology and culture of each eco-region.

Eco-development also recognizes that environmental degradation in the South is the outcome of a particular international economic system, which encourages both the intensive production of cash crops for export and the drive to industrialization. Thus what happens to the environment in the South is clearly linked to the way production, trade and investment processes in the international system operate, as well to the ideology of development, which holds on to the myth of a universalizable pattern of development (W. Sachs, 1992). Eco-development questions the relationships of power in the international system (Redclift, 1987, p. 35). It therefore provides a relevant criticism of the conventional, biocentric and Bruntland sustainability approaches from the perspective of the South.

Summary

The environment is playing an increasingly important role in IR. It has become the issue area in which the independence and sovereignty of communities, states and regions is challenged. *Our Common Future* and UNCED represent the latest testimonies to this, as do continuing attempts to operationalize obligations entered into as a result of these initiatives.

The growing demand for scarce resources, and the pollution generated by increased industrial production and consumption, are often cited as the causes of environmental degradation. However, it is clear that poverty and the lack of alternative livelihoods also contribute to the depletion of resources. 'The crucial question, therefore, is what kind of leverage Southern countries can acquire which will persuade the industrial world that as the original pollutors, they will have to pay if the South is to cooperate in effective environmental control' (Thomas, 1992, p. 18).

The idea of sustainable development is an attempt to eliminate widespread poverty and protect the environment for future generations. There are many tensions apparent in this goal. If sustainable development is to become more than just governmental rhetoric, there are tremendous implications for lifestyles in the North and the South. A consensus must be arrived at which recognizes the differential needs of these two broad groups, as well as those of local communities within them. This is clearly a normative aspiration about how things should be, rather than how they are, the operation of which requires a significant amount of political will; and this will is as yet not evident.

6 The Social Dimension:
Poverty, Population and Hunger

Introduction

Fifty years of development assistance have ensured significant increases in GNP in most of the Third World, yet millions of people in the world still live in poverty. In 1992 it was estimated that about one billion people in the world lived below the World Bank's poverty line of US$370 per year (Belsey, 1992, p. 36), and over half of them lived in South Asia. These startling facts throw into question the whole development debate, which has been overly concerned with the material aspects of economic growth and improvements in national income. In the process it has ignored questions about the quality of life, human security, international justice and equity. The statistics also highlight the fact that there are still tremendous inequalities within the international system.

If development is about improving the quality of people's lives, then we need to know more about what it means to live a meaningful life in a particular context. This will not be the same in all societies. 'The quality of life' refers to more than a quantitative analysis of the living conditions of the poor. It also involves non-material aspects to do with how people are enabled by society to have choices, or to feel emotions. It is not just about having, but also about being.

Furthermore, it is clear that while we may identify the constituents of well-being, it is also important to discuss its realization: under what conditions, national and international, can/

will this occur? While the national context has always been assumed to be the place in which the quality of life can be improved, this is not possible without consideration of the international context. At the international level this requires political commitment. International conventions are signed but not honoured; the need to give at least 0.7 per cent GNP in aid has been recognized but to little effect.[1] There are also questions about targeting aid, and about aid fatigue, which have not been addressed here. More importantly, as the global market plays a role in determining prices and hence the incomes of farmers, it is a key player in the continued existence of hunger.

In this chapter we examine the connections between poverty, population and hunger. The relationship is very much a circular one; there are links of cause and effect between all three. The purpose is to demonstrate these linkages, and to look at the many different ways poor people use what few resources they have to survive. The examples used will mainly be from Sub-Saharan Africa and South Asia, where some of the most concentrated cases of poverty exist. The first section introduces the social dimension of development as a key part of a multifaceted concept. The second section looks at poverty and well-being. The third section examines the question of population, and the final one is about the persistence of hunger in a world in which there is more than enough food.

The social dimension of development

The study of development has been dominated by economics and the assumption that growth, modernization and progress could be measured and relevant comparisons made to see which countries were lacking in development, and how much they needed to catch up. This positive economic methodology is assumed to be both scientific and universal. That is, it is assumed that there is a single, unbiased and universally valid way to measure development. While most social scientists now agree that GNP per capita is a crude and inadequate measure of development, it continues to be used by policy makers (Nussbaum and Sen, 1993).

Yet can we separate the economic quality of our lives – the material aspects – from other aspects of well-being? Should questions of growth and economic stability take precedence over the quality of life? Should wealth be more important than welfare? These are questions which the political economy of development is beginning to address and which shift the emphasis away from questions of economic growth, towards a more multifaceted approach.

In the 1970s the BNA saw a trade-off between social equity and the maximization of GNP. This approach was even adopted by the World Bank under its 1973–80 president, Robert McNamara, to some degree on the basis of the NIEs' experience in achieving high rates of growth along with a fairly equitable distribution of its benefits. The impact of the World Bank's social considerations has, however, been limited and largely symbolic; it has not dislodged the dominant approach, which focuses on economic growth as an indicator of development (Mehmet, 1995).

The World Bank approach to basic needs was based on the assumption that it is possible to identify a universal basket of goods and services which all people should have access to. It is closely related to European development theory in its assumption of a single way of accounting for basic needs. One can argue instead that people's needs differ in different contexts, and thus it is important to situate needs. Much Western aid has been criticized for not taking adequate account of historical and cultural specificities and for not engaging critically with the people it was meant to be helping. In so doing it has ignored ideas about what makes life worth living in particular contexts.

The idea of 'another' development, outlined in chapter 5, embodies the idea that development should stem from the heart of society and be geared towards meeting people's needs, both material and non-material. Measuring or quantifying basic needs is difficult. Sen uses an approach based on the idea of capability and well-being. He views living as 'a combination of various doings and beings with the quality of life to be assessed in terms of the ability to achieve valuable functionings' (A. Sen, 1993, p. 31).

Thus Sen is concerned not simply with adequate nourishment or good health, but also with questions of self-respect and social integration. The point is that development cannot be equated with the achievement of an economic measurement; there are many different understandings of what it means to be poor. Economically poor people may choose to have larger families, or may seek to improve their condition by not engaging with the modern economy. Indeed Sen argues that the freedom to lead different types of life is part of a person's capability set.

Thus it is possible to examine the questions of poverty, population and hunger from two perspectives. We can see them as manifestations of the lack of basic needs and development, or we can seek to ask more meaningful questions about the strategies people employ to survive and to improve the quality of their lives in particular contexts.

Poverty and well-being

What do we mean by poverty? 'There may be as many poor and as many perceptions of poverty as there are human beings' (Rahnema, 1993, p. 158). Poverty is *relative* to different societies and cultural perceptions. What is considered poor in Britain might be considered well off in Haiti; however, people in Britain without adequate income or employment may justifiably believe themselves to be deprived of the basic necessities required for survival. In this sense they would be seen as poor. Following on from this, it is possible to consider that poverty exists in the First as well as the Third World, but has different manifestations in different societies.

Absolute poverty also exists. It is materially evident in the lack of adequate food, sanitation, clean water and access to medical services, and in other forms of hardship (A. Sen, 1981). Absolute poverty may be defined as the inability to meet basic needs such that the quality of life is poor and the ability to meet more secondary needs is limited.[2] It is thus a question of absolute deprivation.

Why, we might ask, do so many people live in such conditions? Poverty is not simply an issue of inequality. Transfers in income from one part of the world to another may reduce the extent of inequality between states, but provide no mechanism for ensuring poverty alleviation. Alternatively, within a given state income may be evenly distributed but everyone might be considered poor.

However, the relationship between poverty and inequality cannot be ignored; indeed one of the striking facts of the postwar international system has been the increased income gap between the poorest and the richest, both within states and between them. In global terms the income disparity between the top quintile (20 per cent) of the world's population and the bottom quintile increased from a ratio of 30:1 in 1969 to 60:1 in 1989 (UNDP, 1992). In absolute terms this translates into an increase in the disparity between the top and bottom quintiles from US$1,864 in 1960 to US$15,149 in 1989. The gap is not only significant, but increasing. Income distribution within countries is also unequal. For example, in Brazil the top quintile of the population receives twenty-six times the income of the bottom quintile (UNDP, 1992). In Tanzania the bottom quintile receives only 6.9 per cent of national income, while the top quintile receives 45.4 per cent (World Bank, 1996).

Poverty is also more complex than having too little money. If it were simply about national income then the dramatic increases in GNP which most parts of the Third World have witnessed might well have eliminated poverty. For example, between 1960 and 1992 the real GNP[3] of the Sub-Saharan region increased from US $934 to $1,346. In India the real GNP per person almost doubled, from US$617 to US$1,230 (UNDP, 1995). However, as was noted in chapter 4, growth does not necessarily reduce poverty, unless it is specifically targeted to do so. GNP says nothing about the distribution of income within a country; it also fails to distinguish between whether the increases are being used to finance education or military spending. Thus there is a need for a more holistic tool for measuring certain indices or aspects of the alleviation of poverty. The United Nations Development Programme (UNDP) HDI is one attempt at this.

Before looking at the HDI we can identify one more problem with using GNP as a measure of development: it can only measure market transactions. Many activities in the Third World take place outside the formal market, through bartering, family labour, community distribution centres, and often illegal activities such as drugs trading. It is also difficult to measure the non-material aspects of poverty such as the lack of choice or political freedom, or the inability to aspire towards a future; these personal aspects may be quantitatively elusive. What is more significant is to ask what resources, material and non-material, people have access to, and how they make use of them in their struggle to survive (Dasgupta, 1993).

The Human Development Index

The need for a more complete measurement of development was recognized by the UNDP in their creation of the HDI in 1990.[4] The HDI, which we looked at briefly in chapter 4, goes beyond the BNA, which provides material goods and services, and seeks to highlight the conditions which are necessary to enlarge people's choices. Once people have access to what the HDI has identified as the three key components of well-being, they will then be better able to make secondary choices. The HDI is thus a composite measurement of three indicators: life expectancy, literacy and purchasing power. The HDI score tells us how far a country has to go in order to arrive at certain specific goals; for life expectancy, this is an average life span of 85 years. The closer a country is to a score of 1, the closer it is to these defined goals and thus the higher the level of human development.

Why did the UNDP chose these three indicators? Life expectancy tells us something about the quality and longevity of life; countries with high life expectancies usually have good health care facilities, in particular primary health care. It is also indicative of a society which cares for its elders. Literacy allows people greater choice of employment, but more importantly it enables people to survive in societies where much is written down. Literacy is also broken down into gender, because too often female education has taken second place to male education. It is now recognized that educating women affects choices about family planning and can thus reduce population pressures. It also allows more women to work outside the home, and this in turn has an impact on family welfare.[5] The third component, income, is not simply per capita income, which is not a useful basis for making cross-country comparisons, but per capita income adjusted for differences in exchange rates and tariffs, as well as for the diminishing utility of higher income to human development. It thus indicates the purchasing power in each country more accurately than does per capita GNP.

Table 6.1 demonstrates that countries, such as Costa Rica, Sri Lanka and Jamaica, can have relatively low per capita incomes yet manage a score relatively high on the HDI. Similarly, Cyprus and Barbados have HDI scores close to many First World countries despite much lower levels of income. This confirms

Table 6.1   Table comparing HDI scores and GNP per capita:
selected countries, 1992

Selected countries	HDI	GNP (US$)
Canada	0.950	20,710
USA	0.938	23,240
Japan	0.936	28,190
UK	0.916	17,790
Cyprus	0.906	9,820
Hong Kong	0.905	15,360
Barbados	0.900	6,540
Costa Rica	0.884	1,960
Jamaica	0.721	1,340
Sri Lanka	0.704	540
China	0.594	470
India	0.439	310
Bangladesh	0.364	220
Ethiopia	0.227	110
Niger	0.207	280

Sources: For HDI scores, UNDP, 1995; for GNP per capita, World
Bank, 1994.

the need for income to be translated into specific measures if
poverty is to be eliminated. Many countries in Sub-Saharan
Africa, however, still have low per capita incomes and low HDI
scores. In terms of regions, the HDI score for Africa is 0.389, less
than half the score of 0.823 for Latin America and the Caribbean.
There is no doubt that growth is an important component of
increasing the HDI score. It is not, though, a sufficient condition.
   The countries which have done exceptionally well on the
HDI, despite relatively low incomes, have done so as a result of
specific public support programmes aimed at improving the
quality of life. From the 1940s Sri Lanka put resources into public
health, increasing its medical personnel from 271 to 664 by 1960.
In 1942 the government also began a programme of providing
free or heavily subsidized rice for the whole population in an
effort to eliminate hunger and malnutrition. The consequences
are evident; by the end of the 1950s Sri Lanka had a life expectancy of 70. By 1960 the death rate had been reduced from 20.6 per

thousand to 8.6 per thousand (Dreze and Sen, 1989). GNP per capita is as low as $540.

Costa Rica has also done extremely well in increasing its HDI score over a short period, although not until the 1960s (see table 6.2). The country benefited from increased revenue in the 1960s from its exports, which allowed for the expansion in welfare services and public support programmes. While revenue has since declined, Costa Rica maintains its near-First World score despite substantially less income. These achievements were made in a country where a high value has traditionally been placed on education; there has been free and compulsory education since 1869. In addition there is a history of democracy, and the army was abolished in 1949.

Table 6.2 Indices of human development in Costa Rica, 1960–80

	Infant mortality	Life expectancy	Fertility rate
1960	76	62.6	7.3
1980	19	72.6	3.7

Source: Dreze and Sen, 1989.

The HDI is not a complete measure of development on its own; it measures only three material indices. One of the major criticisms of it is that it does not look at the political environment of states. It is thus oblivious to the extent of political or civil liberties within a given state. Dasgupta (1993) adds liberty to his index of well-being. Another problem is that in countries such as Costa Rica, the indices are good, but the score does not tell us that the economic system may still be a fairly unequal one, so that there is a need for an active, interventionist welfare state to provide security for the poorest. The HDI should perhaps be complemented with other indices, although it represents a good starting point for assessing the access to resources and the well-being of people in different societies.

Population

The poor have often been accused of overpopulating the world, and more recently of threatening the earth's carrying capacity (Meadows et al., 1974). Malthusian arguments have led to blame for environmental degradation being focused on the Third World, with its high rates of population growth. A reduction in these rates is now seen as an essential component of development.

Like income, population is unevenly distributed both within and between countries. Furthermore, these differences are likely to intensify rather than disappear in the forthcoming years. In South Asia, if the current population growth rate of 2 per cent per annum continues, it is estimated that the total population will reach 1.5 billion by the year 2000. In Sub-Saharan Africa, the population growth rate is even higher at 3 per cent per annum, although most of the region has a low population density (UNDP, 1995). Conversely, population growth rates in the high-income economies are predicted to fall to 0.5 per cent by the year 2000 (World Bank, 1994).

A proper examination of the issue of population, however, does not rely on numbers alone but addresses the questions of why people have large families. The reasons are many and varied. The most frequently cited reason is ignorance or fear of birth control. Yet all societies practise some form of contraception, some better than others (Dasgupta, 1993). The choices people make about children are often regulated by cultural norms; for example, children in Jamaica are viewed as a sign of virility or of womanhood and fertility. There may also be religious reasons for having many children, and/or this may not be perceived as a problem where there are extended family networks of support. The extent to which children are desired is evident in the fact that in areas where life expectancy is as low as 50, women spend a significant percentage of their life in a state of pregnancy, or caring for infants, in the process risking their own lives.[6] These cultural specificities can mean that birth rates may not decrease even if infant mortality rates decline, and that in some cases there may be no causal relationship between the funding of family planning programmes and reductions in birth rates (Duden, 1993).

While ignorance or fear of contraception is rarely a sufficient explanation, not having access to contraception is still a cause for concern. Research by the World Health Organization (WHO) indicates that as many as 120 million women still do not have access to family planning services. This has serious implications in countries where abortion is illegal.

Cultural norms are not the only reason for high birth rates. There is generally an inverse relationship between income and fertility rates. That is, there is a tendency for fertility rates to decrease as incomes increase. Some of the countries with the highest fertility rates – Kenya, Ethiopia, Nepal and Bangladesh – have incomes per head of less than US$1,000 per year. On the other hand, Singapore and Hong Kong, with per capita incomes in excess of US$6,000, have low fertility rates. However, Costa Rica and Chile both have relatively low incomes (US$2,000–3,000 per year) and also low fertility rates. Rising income, when translated into better education, better dietary habits and improved sanitation, usually lowers fertility rates, but there are other factors allied to this.

Dasgupta (1993) introduces considerations of the ways in which poor people seek to survive in situations where access to resources is limited. Having many children can provide a means of security in old age for people who have no job security and where there is no welfare safety net. And, where all children do not survive into adulthood, it may be necessary to have as many as six children to ensure that at least one survives to provide care for the aged. Even when there is a cash income, there may be no reduction in the fertility rate if there is no guarantee of employment. Large families are thus a strategy for survival where income is insecure.

The contribution which children can make to the household is another factor in determining birth rates. In families which eke a living from poor-quality land and to which basic amenities are not readily available, children are often net contributors to the household. They may fetch and carry water, collect firewood, look after smaller children, and perform other such essential activities. A small household is simply not viable in these cases. The children cost little, as they are often undernourished, receive little education, and are clothed at minimal cost. The motivation for children thus springs from the absence of satisfaction of basic needs.

One of the consequences of this is that in some dry land areas in Sub-Saharan Africa, there is a delicate balance between population and environmental degradation. On limited or poor-quality land, even where population–land densities are not high, they may result in soil erosion, loss of soil fertility and/or deforestation. If in addition there are inadequate social facilities, the degradation is likely to include water pollution, disease, malnutrition and infant mortality.

The emphasis on population pressures as a causal factor in environmental degradation shifts the blame away from the distribution of resources within a given state and between states. It may also lead to the conclusion that nothing can be done about poverty. While it is true to say that high birth rates contribute to and may be caused by environmental degradation, poverty and degradation can occur on thinly populated land. More recent research has also found that in parts of Africa, where production processes are extremely labour-intensive, higher population–land ratios are being used to increase rather than decrease productivity (Johnson and Nurick, 1995).

High birth rates are thus a function of a number of factors including cultural norms, lack of access to contraception, low income, lack of job security, limited resources and lack of satisfaction of basic needs. It is still possible to change some of these factors, and the international community does have a role to play here. However, the study of population is not simply a matter of number crunching; there are important considerations of human well-being to be taken into account.

The dimensions of hunger

In Sub-Saharan Africa approximately one third of the region's population (170 million people) have insufficient calories and about 26 million children are malnourished (UNDP, 1995). This occurs despite the fact that in the world as a whole there is sufficient food to offer everyone more than the basic minimum number of calories required per day.

'Silent' or 'invisible' hunger is a term used to refer not so much to famines (which are complete ruptures in food supplies and distribution), but to hunger which is perpetual, and has become almost accepted by the international community as a phenomenon about which little can be done, in spite of the fact that it is by no means inevitable.

Why do so many people go hungry when there is sufficient food to meet their nutritional needs? There are two common answers. One focuses on population–land pressures, the other on entitlements. The former uses Malthusian arguments; that population naturally increases at a faster rate than food production, and consequently overpopulation creates pressure on food supplies, which leads to hunger and starvation. There is thus little which can be done unless population growth rates decline. However, new technologies have enabled food production to outstrip population growth in the world as a whole. Indeed in the EU, farmers have been encouraged to cut back on production levels in recent years. On a global level the problem is not insufficient food, but its uneven distribution.

A. Sen (1981) argues that it is the lack of *entitlement* which causes people to starve. 'Entitlement' refers to the bundle of rights and opportunities available to people, such as money, land or a job. These provide the means by which people can obtain food, as their ability to fulfil their basic calorific needs is linked to their entitlements rather than to overall supplies of food. Food availability is a necessary but not a sufficient condition for satisfying hunger. People still starve, even when food is available.

During the Bengal famine of 1943, there was actually an increase in total food supplies, yet over two million people starved. This was related to a combination of factors such as war, inflation and speculation, so that food prices rose and some people could no longer afford to feed themselves. Others who could afford inflated food prices did not starve. Also, in Bangladesh in 1974, food supplies were at a peak, but people who had lost their jobs starved long before the crops were affected by floods, which then compounded the situation. Thus people go hungry, not because there is insufficient food, but because they have no entitlement to that food (A. Sen, 1981).

Entitlements also raises questions about how food is distributed within households. Often women and children receive less food than men. This is not necessarily related to calorific requirements. One consequence is that 15 per cent of babies are born undernourished in Sub-Saharan Africa, and up to 30 per cent in South Asia. It is now recognized that when food is scarce, women go without. Hence women and children have been identified as vulnerable groups (UNDP, 1995).

It is still the case that most people who regularly go hungry live in the economically poorer regions of the world. There are of course cases of people regularly not meeting their nutritional requirements in the North. However, these are a minority. On average, people in Sub-Saharan Africa receive 67 per cent of the North's daily calorific intake. The corresponding figure for South Asia is 75 per cent. This brings us on to an examination of global patterns of food distribution, or how entitlements are distributed in the global market. This is obviously related to the global system of production and consumption; that is, who produces what, at what price, and who consumes it – what markets exist?

Entitlements in a global context

The traditional model of development has argued that only industry can achieve the increasing returns necessary to finance development. This is evident in both European development theory and the dependency paradigm. It is therefore necessary for countries to make the transition from agriculture to industry. However, the success of this transition depends on the ability of the agricultural sector to generate a surplus which can not only feed the urban labour force, but also be invested in new industries.

The belief that industrialization was the key to transforming so-called 'traditional' economies has led to agriculture being awarded a low priority by governments in Sub-Saharan Africa in the post-independence period. Agriculture has consequently been neglected, the rural sector effectively being taxed in favour of urban development. However, industrialization never really took off in Africa. Although the contribution of industry to GNP increased from 19 per cent in 1965 to 27 per cent in 1987 (World Bank, 1989), this was mainly due to oil extraction and production. There was no major transformation of the production structure of most economies.

The region's share of agriculture in GNP fell from 43 per cent in 1965 to 33 per cent in 1987, but the extent of dependence on commodity exports remained largely unchanged. Primary commodity exports accounted for as much as 88 per cent of total exports for the region in 1987 (World Bank, 1989). Producing commodities for export means that demand and price are determined by the global market. In this way, even the most seemingly remote regions of the world are part and parcel of global agricultural markets.

The implications of cash crop production are many. First, if agriculture is geared for export, there is still the need to feed the local population. This may be done either by the remaining small farms, or through imports of food. Usually the two exist together, but if food imports are cheaper than locally produced food, this will tip the balance in their favour. One consequence of this has been the drive away from production for local consumption – that is, subsistence agriculture – towards production for global markets – that is, cash crops.

There is nothing inherently bad in cash crop production; or to put it another way, there is nothing inherently good in being totally self-sufficient. A country which is self-sufficient in food need not go hungry; however, it may not have access to other basic necessities, such as energy to generate heat or light. And self-sufficiency does not guarantee that nutritional requirements are met, although it is a good starting point.

The benefits of self-sufficiency are greatest when market conditions are unstable. Unfortunately (and this is the subject of the following chapter), the market for agricultural exports has historically been unstable at best and non-profitable at worst. Thus if the price of coffee is low relative to other goods, those who produce coffee for export will suffer a decrease in income and consequently, in the extreme, a lack of entitlement to the satisfaction of basic needs including adequate food.

While there is no inevitability in the equation, in Sub-Saharan Africa food production per head has decreased in the past two decades. China has solved the problem of chronic undernourishment and India has managed to avoid famine since independence (Dreze and Sen, 1989); yet in the 1980s only 25 per cent of Africans lived in countries where food consumption per capita was increasing, and this represents a decline since the 1970s from about 65 per cent (World Bank, 1989). The prevalence of hunger and recurring famine has increased despite the objectives of the Lagos Plan of Action for the continent to be self-sufficient in food production by the year 2000 (Ofuatey-Kodjoe, 1991).

The problem of food insecurity in Africa is thus becoming increasingly severe. Part of the reason lies in the disproportionately large investment in research in export crops compared to that for food crops (Platteau, 1991). This is a legacy of a colonial system geared to the production of commodities for export, and to this end there have been significant applications of science-based agriculture to crops such as cocoa, coffee, palm oil, cotton and ground nuts. Platteau argues that if the same amount of research had gone into traditional food crops, similar success, in terms of increased yields for example, could be achieved.

The growing dependence on food imports has reduced the income of the rural poor. Its causes can be traced both to poor performance in the agricultural sector (leading to calls for more intensive practices and rapid technological advances) and also to the policies of taxing the agricultural sector.

There may be little improvement in the price of commodity exports, even with the Uruguay Round of GATT negotiations. Measures are to be taken to ensure the poorest net food importers do not suffer disproportionately (see chapter 7). It is nevertheless still the case that people's livelihoods depend, at the most basic level, on being able to feed themselves.

Summary

Poverty, population and hunger are all related crises of development. The existence of poverty is a causal factor in hunger, and inadequate nutrition does not enable one to climb out of the poverty trap. Similarly, people have children not because they do not know any better, but as a means of survival when resources are scarce.

More importantly, we have pointed out that national income can only ever be a partial measure of development; poverty is not simply a matter of too little money, and hunger is not merely a result of too little food. There are distributional factors which need to be taken into account. The continued existence of poverty and its manifestations is evidence that development, as it has been conceived to date, has not been able to address adequately some of the most fundamental problems facing parts of the Third World today. Thus the Independent Commission on Population and Quality of Life (1996, p. 16) has called for 'a new synthesis, a new balance between market, society and environment, between efficiency and equity, between wealth and welfare. A new balance between economic growth on the one hand and social harmony and sustainability on the other'. That is, we need to place social development at the centre of policy making, rather than economic growth and competition.

7 | International Commodity Trade and Development

Introduction

This chapter looks at the political economy of international commodity trade, a key issue for many Third World states. European development theory has viewed trade as the 'engine of growth', the means by which the 'less developed economies' could become developed. This view is echoed in the prevailing liberal world view that (free) trade is the generator of world prosperity, particularly when goods and services are exchanged on the basis of comparative advantage (Tussie, 1987). The dependency perspective, on the other hand, initially viewed trade as detrimental to development; incorporation into world markets would only lead to more underdevelopment. Indeed the Third World bloc created the United Nations Conference on Trade and Development (UNCTAD) as an alternative to the liberal GATT.

Trade has thus played a key role in development theories. However, the assumptions upon which these are based are now questioned by the increasing diversity of Third World interests. It is also clear that international trade has significant negative effects: environmental destruction and widening gaps between the rich and the poor, within and between societies, as well as new efforts to impose inappropriate or politically counter-productive standards on the poorer Third World (Hettne, 1995a).

The first section of this chapter looks at current trends in international commodity trade: who trades and in what quantities? Is the dependency thesis about declining terms of trade for primary commodities a valid one? In the second section we examine how the market for commodities is regulated, if at all. One recurring and important theme is the instability of agricultural markets, which in turn implies instability in income. How do states which depend on agricultural markets try to circumvent this instability? The third section looks at the Uruguay Round of negotiations in GATT as another step in the process of global economic liberalism, and one of which the more economically advanced Third World states have become strong supporters. In particular, the negotiations for agricultural reform demonstrate the distinct livelihoods at stake. Throughout the chapter two common assumptions are examined: that the Third World produces most agricultural commodities, and that the Third World is in favour of non-market mechanisms and preferential treatment in agricultural trade. The chapter thus questions the assumption that the Third World has a common interest where commodities are concerned.

International commodity trade

A commodity is simply an article of trade. It usually refers to primary products or raw materials; that is, to unprocessed products. This includes minerals, metals and fuel, as well as agricultural and food products. In this chapter we are primarily concerned with agricultural commodities; for example, sugar, coffee or wheat. Markets for agricultural commodities are among the most unstable as well as the most protected. The arguments for protecting agriculture vary from country to country; however, the primary concern in the North and the South seems to be about food security – feeding one's population is seen as crucial to the security of the state.

The volume and direction of commodity trade

As table 7.1 shows, there has been a tendency to move away from the production and consumption of commodities since the 1970s (Finlayson and Zacher, 1988).

This has occurred for a number of reasons. The action of OPEC

Table 7.1 Percentage of world exports, 1970 and 1992

Commodity	1970	1992
All commodities	36	25
Non-fuel, minerals, metals	20	13

Source: World Bank, 1994.

in the 1970s changed the face of commodity markets significantly and irreversibly. The fact that a group of Third World producers were effectively able to hold the world to ransom through their actions frightened the North into intensifying existing trends towards self-sufficiency. There has consequently been a slowdown in the growth of markets in the North, especially in the EU, which accounts for half the world's primary commodity imports.

Since the price boom in 1973–5, there has also been a downward trend in world commodity prices, reducing incentives for countries to engage in or increase their share of world commodity trade. Exporters and importers are now more acutely aware of the smallest price changes. Producers have, where possible, diversified their production structures so that they no longer rely solely on the export of primary commodities. Consumers have learnt to conserve and recycle commodities where possible. Technological changes have led to the development of a number of synthetic substitutes; for example, artificial sweeteners to replace sugar, which has significant implications for the producers of sugar.

Nevertheless, commodity trade is still a significant percentage of world trade. In the World Bank's high-income economies group, most exports are of industrial products; however, about 18 per cent of total exports are raw materials (including fuels). Within this there are vast extremes; for some countries such as Australia, primary commodities account for 65 per cent of exports. Likewise in Norway the corresponding figure is 68 per cent of exports. In the low-income economies group the corresponding figure is 38 per cent of total exports, and in middle-income economies it is 51 per cent (World Bank, 1994).

It is commonly assumed that the South exports primary commodities to the North, and imports manufactures in return;

likewise that the North exports manufactures to the South, and imports primary commodities. However, such an assumption needs qualification. First, we need to make the distinction between agricultural commodities and fuels, metals and minerals. Second, there is the distinction between the industrial South and non-industrialized Third World states. We have already (in chapter 4) examined the case of the NIEs of East Asia. The four NIEs we looked at were by and large importers of agricultural products; or net food importers, and exporters of industrial products. It is possible to argue that they are exceptions and that they no longer fit into the category of Third World states; certainly they are no longer low-income economies. However, many other Third World countries, for example in Latin America, have expanded their manufacturing base while decreasing their reliance on primary commodities as a source of income (see table 7.2).

Table 7.2 Change in percentage share of exports of agricultural commodities, 1970–92

Economy	1970	1992
High-income economies	16	11
Low-income economies	44	17
Sub-Saharan Africa	46	32
South Asia	44	21
Latin America & Caribbean	45	30

Source: World Bank, 1994.

This process of industrial expansion represents a marked change from the 1970s, when primary commodities accounted for over 80 per cent by value of Third World exports. In the low- and middle-income economies, manufactures now constitute approximately 52 per cent of total exports (this includes the NIEs), while unprocessed agricultural commodities excluding fuel account for only 18 per cent of exports. If we add fuel exports to this the total is still less than manufactures, at 47 per cent. However, it should be noted that nearly half of the total Third World export of manufactures can be accounted for by the NIEs of East Asia (World Bank, 1994).

The aggregate figures obviously conceal significant differences between Third World states, and there remain many low-income economies, especially in South Asia and Sub-Saharan Africa, which still rely on the export of primary commodities for a substantial percentage of their national income. In 1983 the UN estimated that in the South, fifty countries still depended on primary commodity exports for at least 70 per cent of their foreign exchange, excluding oil (Finlayson and Zacher, 1988). In addition, these states probably produce only a narrow range of commodities and are thus extremely vulnerable to price fluctuations (see table 7.3).

Table 7.3   Percentage GNP from agriculture, 1992

Economy	%
High-income economies	4
Low-income economies	29
Sub-Saharan Africa	20
South Asia	32
Latin America & Caribbean	12

Source: World Bank, 1994.

Even when the quantity of primary commodities exported is small, the number of people employed in the sector may still be substantial. In Africa the percentage of the labour force employed in agriculture between 1982 and 1984 was as high as 78 per cent. The corresponding figure for Asia was 71 per cent (World Bank, 1986). In the First World the figure is less than 10 per cent. Thus while the size of the involvement in world trade may be small, the importance of primary commodities to the domestic economy is significant in terms of income and employment.

The declining terms of trade debate

In chapter 6 we noted the transition from subsistence production to production for export as having the potential to increase export earnings. This of course depends on, among other things, what price commodity exports can command.

In the 1960s ECLA and the dependency school argued that reliance on the export of primary commodities consigned the Third World to a state of perpetual poverty, because there was a tendency for the terms of trade for primary commodities to decline over time (see chapter 3).

Spraos (1980) found that Prebisch (1950) had relied on very limited data, mainly for the UK, and did not in fact distinguish between primary commodities from the First World and from the Third World. While a deteriorating trend for Third World primary commodity exports was noticeable in the data, it was much smaller than was suggested by Prebisch.

In addition, the limited period which Prebisch reviewed (1870–1938) included a world depression and a world war. These two aberrations skewed the data significantly and made the hypothesis less plausible. Spraos thus points out that while it is possible to say that there has been a persistent deterioration in the terms of trade for primary commodities (excluding oil in 1973) relative to manufactures since 1945, there are many question marks over such a claim. For example, what period of review was covered by the statistics, in what year did it start and when did it finish, were there any wars or droughts which disrupted prices, what index of prices was used, which primary commodities were included and which manufactures? Up to 1970, primary commodity prices have had many ups and downs, but on average have done better than in the pre-1945 period. The claim for a deterioration in the terms of trade can only be made over a short period of time. The thesis thus has limited validity as a general explanation.

Besides, if a short-run deterioration in the terms of trade can be identified, this may not always be a bad thing. It may be that productivity is increasing, and less inputs can produce the same outputs, thereby decreasing the cost of production. This would be considered more efficient production in liberal economic theory. The World Bank estimated that the terms of trade for the NICs declined by more than 16 per cent between 1980 and 1988, yet this was compensated for by a huge increase in demand for their products. Likewise since the 1970s there has been an increase in agricultural productivity associated with Green Revolution policies,[1] which has lowered the cost of producing certain crops, mainly wheat, corn and rice, so that the price of these commodities has also fallen.

It is nevertheless true that if the price of imports increases, and exports do not increase proportionately, those countries which rely on imports are placed in a difficult position. This was precisely what happened to many oil-importing Third World states when the price of oil increased in 1973. In many cases this resulted in increased indebtedness as countries borrowed in order to finance imports. Despite its shortcomings, the terms of trade debate drew attention to the relationship between trade and development and the extremely vulnerable position in which many Third World states still find themselves.

What is less debatable is that the prices of primary commodities fluctuate more than the prices of industrial products, and this means that income also fluctuates. These fluctuations can be seen in table 7.4. The indices show the average deviation from the price in any particular year. Thus for cocoa in the period 1974–84 the price in a typical year was 34 per cent above or below the trend for that particular year. The fluctuations in sugar prices were as high as 90 per cent in the period 1964–8.

Table 7.4 Price instability in commodities, selected years

Commodity	1964–8	1974–84
Sugar	90.8	51.5
Cocoa	37.3	34.1
Rice	33.0	21.9
Coffee	32.0	37.7
Wheat	24.3	16.9
Tea	21.7	23.6
Beef	16.7	11.3
Cotton	14.3	10.7

Source: World Bank, 1986.

The reasons for such substantial fluctuations are many; agricultural products are obviously subject to changes in climatic conditions, their output is often seasonal, and prices vary depending on whether they are in season or not. Furthermore, despite large price fluctuations, because of the nature of production, supply and demand are less responsive in the short run to

changes in price. A similar table for price fluctuation of manufactures reveals a deviation of usually less than 10 per cent, but
never greater than 20 per cent (World Bank, 1986).

Free trade or protection?

Agriculture is central to the interests of the rich industrial states,
where it is often heavily subsidized. It is also still important to
the poorer non-industrialized states, where it is often taxed, and
is the principal source of export earnings. This section examines
the tensions between the liberal assumptions about the inherent
goodness of free trade based on increasing interdependence
between economies, and alternative perspectives which question the neutrality of the market, and call for mechanisms to
circumvent it.

The liberal regime

The conduct of international trade has been closely monitored
by governments and international organizations since 1945.
The idea of an international trade organization (ITO) to monitor
and regulate international trade led to the establishment of
GATT in 1947. Although GATT was designed as a pro-
visional instrument, it subsequently became the principal
framework for multilateral trade negotiations (MTNs) between
its members.

The idea behind GATT is the liberal assumption that free trade
is the generator of world prosperity. GATT therefore seeks to
reduce, as far as possible, all barriers to trade, in particular non-
tariff barriers, as well as to eliminate discriminatory treatment in
trading relations.

There are four key principles which govern the activities of
GATT:

1 non-discrimination – all trading states should be accorded
  equal treatment, or, in GATT terminology, all states should be
  treated as though they were the most favoured nation (MFN);
2 reciprocity of preferential treatment – if country A agrees to
  lower its tariffs against country B by 10 per cent, country B
  should reciprocate in an equivalent manner;

3 transparency – any barriers to trade should be in the form of tariffs, which are a visible mechanism of protectionism; GATT does not approve of non-tariff barriers (NTBs) to imports such as quotas, or high qualitative (health and safety) requirements;
4 an on-going agenda of reducing tariffs by engaging in MTNs (M. Williams, 1994).

It is obvious from the above that GATT does not in fact apply the principle of unrestricted free trade, but allows a certain amount of domestic protection; for example, the creation of customs unions and free trade areas between groups of states on clearly defined terms. Also GATT allows certain preferential agreements for developing countries, including the Generalized System of Preferences (GSP). GATT is thus not so much the defender of free trade, as the facilitator of managed trade. While free trade is held up as an ideal, GATT defends a mixture of multilateralism and bilateralism. That is, it facilitates not only agreements between all parties to the GATT, but also agreements between two parties, and more recently between groups of states, such as the EU.

GATT, as the regulator of world trade, also reflects the structures of power in the world economy. GATT was originally considered by the developing countries as instrumental in expanding the trade and prosperity of the First World to the exclusion of the Third. The post-1945 increase in trade has indeed favoured the North, with its share of the value of world trade increasing from 65 per cent in 1950 to 80 per cent in 1970. In contrast the South's share has decreased from 35 per cent to 20 per cent in the same period (Tussie, 1987). It is debatable to what extent GATT alone has been responsible for this;[2] nevertheless, the reality of declining trade has prompted criticism of both the operation and principles of GATT from the Third World.

In terms of operational procedures, negotiations in GATT usually take place between the principal buyers and sellers of products. This invariably means the more economically powerful nations set the agendas of GATT. Or, to put it another way, those states which contribute significant market shares to world trade in particular products can influence the outcome of negotiations on those products in their favour. Small traders have to accept the conditions the larger traders determine.

In terms of principles, GATT defends a system of trade which assumes all trading partners are equal. The South, on the other hand, has argued that this is unfair, as it cannot compete on equal terms with the North. The South has nevertheless also criticized the manner in which the North evades GATT regulations and prevents market access for Southern products. The South has thus called for *special and differential* treatment within GATT; that is, for the removal of the obligation to grant reciprocal tariff concessions and permission to protect its domestic markets, as well as for special access to markets in the North.

One concession to Third World demands for special and differential treatment was the creation in 1971 of the GSP.[3] This grants preferential access to First World markets for Third World manufactures, and was designed as an attempt to assist in the industrialization of the Third World. However, the GSP does not cover textiles, which is the easiest industry to begin the industrialization process with. Furthermore, the preferences granted vary from country to country and from product to product. Indeed many products are excluded from First World markets if deemed to be harmful to their domestic interests.

Futures markets

In recognition of the instability which characterizes commodity markets, one means of stabilizing income (and certainly one which is favoured by those against market interventions) is through organized *futures markets*. Developed in the nineteenth century, a futures market provides buyers and sellers with insurance against violent price fluctuations.

In futures markets, producers and consumers interact through a futures dealer. The buyers determine specific quantities of particular commodities which they intend to purchase at a specific price, and the sellers secure for themselves a market for their crops, before the harvest. Any risk involved is effectively shouldered by the dealer. The International Commodities Clearing House (ICCH), which allows complete exchangeability between contracts and extreme flexibility in trading, provides the dealer with the assurance that the contract will be fulfilled.

Futures markets can offer more security for growers, reducing the uncertainty of markets, without trying to control prices. They also offer a guarantee against exchange rate fluctuations, which are increasingly a feature of trade. One limitation is that futures markets are not particularly good at predicting future prices, and consequently it is difficult to secure a market more than eighteen months in advance. Furthermore, like all free markets they provide no guarantee that the price obtained will be sufficient to cover costs, much less to ensure a minimum standard of living. Thus for those whose very survival depends on the income secured from commodity exports, they provide no guarantees.

Futures markets have not developed to the extent that their (liberal) supporters expected. There is little research on or development of them, and they cover only a small percentage of total commodity trade. They certainly have not kept pace with the increasingly complex manner in which trade in agricultural commodities is conducted.

Alternative forms of management

Because the South has perceived its interests to be marginal in GATT, it has made use of alternative forums in which it has more influence. It has made various attempts, mainly through UNCTAD, to restructure world trade by changing the rules, regulations and premises upon which it is based, as well as to regulate and control trade by means of commodity agreements.[4] These incursions into the market are based on the assumption that the Third World needed protection in order to industrialize, particularly in relation to commodities because of the inherent instability in commodity markets. This section examines some of the attempts which have been made to alter and regulate commodity trade. One such attempt was the call for a NIEO in the 1970s.

The NIEO On the basis of the success of OPEC in 1973, and despite the fact that many Third World states suffered a great deal because of the oil price increases, the South felt it could use this new-found commodity power as a bargaining tool with the North. The NIEO was a largely unsuccessful attempt by the

South to restructure the international economic order in its favour. The demands were comprehensive and wide ranging.

The underlying approach may be divided into two broad strands. One section views the new order as a means of providing exemptions for the South from existing rules of the world economy (such as reciprocity in GATT), along with increased aid and trade provisions. The South would thus benefit from special concessional arrangements. The other strand sees the NIEO as a means to achieve more radical, long-term change in the international system, such as the redistribution of political and economic power. The precise details of the NIEO demands are extensive but not the subject of this chapter. It is sufficient to point out that in the end, and almost inevitably, there were no radical changes to structures of power. Instead a few minor compromises from the North were gained. One such concession was the creation of the Common Fund for Commodities.

The Integrated Programme for Commodities and the Common Fund The tendency for the price of primary commodities, especially agricultural ones, to vary more than the price of manufactures means that for those who depend on commodity trade export earnings fluctuate, and long-term economic planning is difficult. In order to counteract this, the South focused its attention on trying to stabilize prices and fluctuations in earnings, and also to implement schemes which would help insure against shortfalls in export receipts. A key part of the NIEO demands was the creation of an Integrated Programme for Commodities. On the assumption of declining terms of trade, the IPC sought to stabilize and improve prices of a number of key primary commodities, including food, minerals and agricultural goods, through the creation of as many international commodity agreements (ICAs) as possible.

The IPC also sought to create a Common Fund to finance buffer stocks of key commodities to help stabilize prices. The assumption behind the Common Fund was that one of the primary obstacles to new ICAs was the lack of finance available for such stocks. However, the potential cost of such a fund was not supported by the major economies, especially the USA (Finlayson and Zacher, 1988). The Common Fund, much reduced in financial terms, was finally agreed in 1980, although it was not ratified until 1989 (Corea, 1992). Recent analysis suggests that 'while the Common Fund will never perform the role originally intended as stockpile banker, it could become a practical source of technical assistance for developing countries on the development and marketing of commodities' (Corea, 1992, p. 105).

While the Common Fund negotiations took place, UNCTAD was also discussing the creation of ICAs for eighteen key commodities. By 1976, however, commodity prices had fallen and the bargaining leverage of the commodity producers had declined. The only new ICA to emerge from the negotiations was one for rubber in 1977.

International Commodity Agreements ICAs are agreements between exporters and importers of a particular commodity. They attempt to regulate supply by the use of buffer stocks (if the commodity can be stored), and to maintain prices in an agreed range through the use of export quotas. Their success depends on the compliance of the major producers of the commodity. If large producers do not wish to join, the agreement becomes ineffective. Similarly, all producers need to be committed to the success of the agreement, so that when prices rise they are not tempted to dump their supplies on the world market. ICAs thus demand a certain amount of unity among producers. While this was possible with OPEC initially, it is perhaps less possible with commodities produced by a large number of countries.

There have been few successful ICAs. That is, few ICAs have been able to achieve their objective of price stabilization for any length of time. International commodity agreements can, when effective, keep prices within a specified range, although they cannot eliminate price fluctuations. They have not, however, been the favoured method of regulation with the North. Indeed the collapse of the International Tin Agreement in 1985 with a large debt has perhaps dealt a death blow to future ICAs.

Two case studies

The exceptional case of OPEC The best-known example of a commodity agreement is that of OPEC. In the 1970s OPEC was influential in changing the thinking of commodity producers about their ability to influence commodity prices. Indeed the success of OPEC led to the call for more producers' associations to be formed. However, the case of oil cannot be generalized for all other primary commodities. The demand for oil is fairly inelastic in the short run; there are no ready substitutes, and it is difficult to reduce consumption rapidly. At the time (1973) there were a limited number of producers, who had a common interest in securing higher prices for their product. Through strong leadership and this common interest they were able to limit the supply of oil and force a price rise. However, OPEC's success was short-lived; new sources of oil were found and substitutes for oil-based energy were developed. In addition the unity of the group did not survive periods of low prices.

The International Sugar Agreement   Sugar is a commodity which is produced in the South and the North. In the South, earnings from sugar exports amounted to US$8 billion per year in the period 1980–2. Indeed 65 per cent of total world market exports originate in the South (FAO, 1995). However, the two biggest exporters in the 1980s were the EU and Australia.

There have been attempts to regulate the world sugar market since 1937. Up until the early 1960s the agreement was fairly successful in avoiding sharp fluctuations, but in 1961 it was abandoned, when the USA ended its policy of importing Cuban sugar. Cuba was at this time one of the largest sugar producers. Without its usual market, exports of Cuban sugar on the world market would have caused a severe fall in prices. The USSR agreed to buy the displaced Cuban sugar in a special agreement, but it was too late to prevent disruption in world market prices.

By this time there were an increasing number of sugar-exporting states. Compliance from all of them would have been necessary for an effective agreement. The US decision not to buy Cuban sugar marked the beginning of a series of special or preferential agreements for sugar. In addition to the USSR agreement to buy Cuban sugar, the EU created a preferential trading arrangement with the African, Caribbean and Pacific (ACP) group of states in 1975,[5] and the USA established its own import quota system.

Subsequent attempts to establish an effective agreement have met with little success. The EU for its part has been unwilling to restrict its world market exports in line with proposed quotas. It is difficult to conclude an agreement without the consent of one of the major players. Also, preferential bilateral agreements effectively bypass the world market and make it difficult for any new International Sugar Agreement to be effective.[6] The agreement can have little influence on the world market because an increasing quantity of sugar – 75 per cent (FAO, 1995) – is not traded on the open market.

From special and differential treatment to embracing the market

The Third World as a bloc has been the principal advocate of intervention in commodity markets. It was its members' efforts, through UNCTAD, the NIEO and OPEC, which were responsible for the prominence of commodity issues on the international agenda in the 1970s. However, by the late 1980s members of what used to be the Third World coalition were calling for reform of the world trading system in favour of more liberal markets. How and why did this complete turn-round occur?

In the 1960s and 1970s the Third World, on the basis of the dependency paradigm, articulated in practically a unified manner the view that integration into the world economy on equal terms would lead to the disintegration of the domestic economy. Domestic industries had to be protected and access to markets had to be on preferential terms. The South consistently appealed for, and won, special and differential trading arrangements.

The North, on the other hand, had established a system, under the leadership of the USA and based on liberal principles, for dismantling trade barriers. GATT was intended to increase world trade and prosperity through the market. However, by the 1980s the Third World's share of exports had fallen dramatically. Between 1981 and 1986 all but the NIEs in East Asia had experienced severe recession and negative growth rates.

The debt crisis which erupted in the Third World in the 1980s fundamentally changed its approach to trade policy. The need for export revenue to service the debt prompted a reconsideration of how best to achieve this aim. Many countries in the Third World have consequently reduced their trade barriers (often independently of GATT), in part as an attempt to emulate the NIEs' success, but also because the major lending institutions, namely the IMF and the World Bank, firmly insisted upon *structural adjustment* of Third World economies.[7] This involved, among other things, the liberalization of trade policy. Government price-support programmes and import restrictions were discouraged. Combined with currency devaluations, this has created more open and externally oriented economies, in line with neo-liberal prescriptions. Thus by the 1980s 'developing countries stepped to the vanguard of trade liberalization as a growing number of countries undertook a fundamental change of direction towards a greater degree of openness' (Tussie and Glover, 1993, p. 1).

The significance of this change should not be underrated, in terms of either the sometimes harsh domestic effects of structural adjustment or of the effect on world markets. Today, many countries, for example in Latin America, have more open trade regimes than the North. Previous scepticism of GATT has been replaced with more active interest from and participation by the Third World. Those countries which have managed to attain some level of industrialization are keen to ensure access to important markets in the North. Similarly, large agricultural exporters in the Third World, again for example in Latin America, are concerned with access to large agricultural markets in the North.

However, having finally accepted that free markets are beneficial to development, the South encountered high levels of protectionism in the North. This protectionism is characterized by its reliance on NTBs to trade, and an increasing number of bilateral and free trade agreements (FTAs) designed to manage or limit imports from the Third World (Tussie and Glover, 1993). These arrangements effectively bypass the GATT principle that one should treat all states as though they were MFNs, and limit GATT's ability to regulate trade.

GATT's main achievements have been in the trade of manufactured products. To this extent it has served the industrial nations well, as the products which have benefited most from trade liberalization are produced by the North. Implicitly it has also served the interests of TNCs which produce these goods. However, until the Uruguay Round of GATT negotiations neither agriculture nor textiles was part of GATT's activities. Thus substantial amounts of trade, important to the South, have fallen outside of the scope of GATT.

The Uruguay Round and Third World interests

The USA has always been ambivalent about the liberalization of agricultural trade, although at times it has intervened to promote price stability for exports and food aid for the Third World. While supporting liberalization and multilateralism in world trade policy generally, in agriculture the US has claimed special interests. As the principal power in the post-war international system, its position has been determining.

In 1955 the USA applied for and was granted a waiver from GATT principles in order to protect its domestic farm programme by the use of import quotas. There was no time limit to this waiver. As the USA was the largest producer and exporter of agricultural foodstuffs, the waiver prevented GATT from trying to regulate agricultural trade. The 1955 waiver also set a precedent, which was followed in 1958 by the creation of the Common Agricultural Policy (CAP), designed to protect and support farm incomes in the EU. With two such exclusions it became clear that there was no possibility of GATT regulating trade in agriculture. Thus where agriculture is concerned, instead of states having to bring their domestic sectors in line with GATT requirements, GATT rules have been written to fit whatever domestic agricultural programmes the major powers establish (Avery, 1993).

There have of course been attempts to get agriculture on the GATT agenda, but until the 1986 Punte del Este meeting, which launched the Uruguay Round of GATT negotiations, these were largely unsuccessful. However, the determining impetus for reform came not from the South, but from the USA. Thus agriculture became a key component of the GATT negotiations because the US decided to make it one.

In understanding the negotiations for agriculture in the Uruguay Round, it is important to note that once agriculture was on the agenda there were effectively three major players: the USA, the EU and the Cairns Group. Whereas previously GATT decisions were taken by US leadership, and later with the EU and Japan, in the Uruguay Round this changed. The Cairns Group became a third force, and one which could not be ignored, in the war between EU and US interests.

The Cairns Group

The Cairns Group is particularly interesting because it cuts across traditional North–South divisions. The establishment of the Cairns Group demonstrates that by the late 1980s, in contrast to the 1970s, there was no single Third World position on agricultural trade. The members of the Cairns Group were all large exporters of agricultural commodities, which immediately excluded the interests of those Third World states which are net food importers (Africa, Asia).

It is commonly assumed that the only way for weak states to influence international negotiations is by forming coalitions, effectively grouping together to outnumber the strong states. While coalitions of similarly situated states are more common, the Cairns Group represented a transregional coalition of Northern and Southern states. Furthermore, unlike OPEC or other ICAs, their interests were not in one commodity which might only appeal to a few states, but in one specific but potentially wide-ranging area: agriculture.

Led by Australia, the Cairns group consisted of New Zealand, Fiji, Indonesia, Malaysia, the Philippines, Thailand, Argentina, Brazil, Chile, Colombia, Uruguay, Canada and Hungary. Some of these are middle-income and others are low-income states. What they have in common is that they are all major agricultural exporters, and between them they play an important role in tropical and temperate agricultural markets, including cereals,

Table 7.5 Percentage market shares in selected agricultural commodities, 1985

Commodity	Cairns	EU	USA
Maize	19	26	40
Wheat	42	23	25
Meat	24	57	8
Dairy	11	72	3
Rice	33	17	20
Sugar	15	14	1
Coffee	37	5	1

Source: Tussie and Glover, 1993.

coffee, rice, rubber, wheat, wool, animal foodstuffs and vegetable oils (see table 7.5).

Agriculture in the Uruguay Round

The discussion of agriculture in GATT was prompted by what amounted to a competition between the EU and the USA to award higher and higher subsidies to their farm sectors in an effort to gain a greater share of the world market. By the end of the 1970s, the EU had changed from being a net importer of agricultural products to being the second largest exporter. The Cairns Group was formed in 1986 to pressure the US and the EU to end the export subsidy war. They claimed that Cairns Group exports had been adversely affected by the policies of the EU and the USA, in particular by export subsidies. The members of the Cairns Group could not afford the same extent of subsidies, especially the severely indebted Latin American states.

In response to the Cairns Group's criticisms, the US submitted to GATT a proposal for reforming and liberalizing agricultural trade. The initial position of the USA was to demand an absolute phasing out of all barriers to access, the conversion of all NTBs into tariffs and the gradual reduction of these, and an end to all domestic subsidies over a ten-year period. This was a complete turn-round from the US policy of protecting its agricultural sector.

However, the US dramatically underestimated the opposition which would arise from the EU. The EU was not prepared to reform its CAP in line with external demands. The value of the CAP to the EU was more than just economic; it fulfilled important social and ecological functions. Importantly also, because agriculture plays a different role in each EU member state, it has consistently proved difficult to obtain a consensus on CAP reform, much less a complete overhaul (Ritson and Harvey, 1996).

The Cairns Group was also calling for reform in agriculture, in particular reform of the CAP. They did not want the negotiations to end up as a bilateral agreement between the EU and the USA, or for agriculture to be left out of the final agreement (Tussie, 1993). Some members even threatened to block agreements in other areas if no agreement was reached in agriculture. Nevertheless the Cairns Group position, which called for more gradual and less severe reductions in support, represented a middle way between the zero-option position of the USA and the intransigence of the EU.

Negotiations on agriculture were deadlocked in 1990. The EU was unwilling to change its position, and the USA and the Cairns Group eventually threatened to pull out of all other negotiations unless there was an agreement on agriculture. The EU began internal reforms in 1990/1, although insisting this was due not to the GATT but to domestic budgetary pressures. The negotiations thus resumed in 1991, by which time the positions of the three groups were closer together. Eventual agreement was reached in December 1993.

The assumption behind reform in agricultural trade practice was that by cutting domestic support measures, through which farmers in the USA and EU receive higher than world market prices for their produce, world agricultural prices would rise, thus affording those who depend on agricultural exports a better income. With the reduction of tariff barriers and NTBs to trade, market access would improve and there would be an increase in total agricultural trade, again improving the income of agricultural exporters. However, if prices rise, those countries which import food will have to pay more. Thus it was clear that food-producing countries with a competitive export sector would gain, but food-importing countries would probably be net losers (M. Williams, 1994).

An important distinction needs to be made here between temperate commodities and tropical agricultural commodities. By and large, the highest levels of export subsidies existed in the EU and the USA for mainly temperate products; in particular wheat, meat and dairy products. Consequently the debates in GATT were mainly about reducing the rates of subsidy in temperate agricultural commodities. Tropical products were not part of the debate between the EU and the USA. The Cairns Group, however, included countries which were mainly large exporters of tropical products, such as rice, sugar and coffee, and which wanted access to the EU market for these products on the same terms as those offered through the Lomé Convention to the ACP group of states. While the Cairns Group would have had to face higher prices for their temperate food imports, they nevertheless wanted tropical products to be included in the debate.

There remained a significant group of Third World agricultural importers, of cereals, meat and dairy produce, whose interests the Cairns Group could not represent, and outside the group there was no consistent negotiating position from the Third World. The difficulty was that many Third World countries both import food and export cash crops. Take for example the case of India, a major agricultural producer, but also an importer of wheat. Similarly, Jamaica exports unrefined sugar to the UK and the USA, but then imports the refined product back. It was difficult to identify any single Third World interest which could form a negotiating position. Without a common position, the South as a group could have little influence on the outcome of the negotiations (Hopkins, 1993).

A small group of net food importers did get together to argue for compensation for poorer food-importing countries. The group, known as the W74, under the leadership of Jamaica, was composed of Egypt, Mexico, Morocco and Peru (Mexico eventually joined the Cairns Group). While these states opposed liberalization, because a significant percentage of their income is spent on importing food, many also stood to gain from the removal of barriers to trade and the opening up of Northern markets. The only unifying factor among them was the insistence on concessions and differential treatment for the least developed countries. Consequently the group's ability to influence the proceedings was severely limited by their conflicting interests.

The changes in the GATT negotiations are significant. Since the 1970s, GATT principles of multilateralism and non-discrimination have been gradually eroded, prompting numerous calls for reform of world trade. Allied to this has been the decline in the role of the US as leader of the system. Although the post-war international system was established on the assumption of this role, the US has been increasingly unable to take decisions without consulting the EU and Japan. The entry of the Cairns Group as a major player in the agricultural negotiations was certainly unprecedented, but again highlighted the need for reform of the system.

The final agreement

Agreement was finally reached in December 1993. The final agreement makes important distinctions between the developed, the developing and the least developed countries. Developed countries have six years to complete the changes. Developing countries have more time to adjust (ten years), they are required to make smaller reductions, and can be more flexible in setting tariff reductions. The least developed countries are required to make no reductions. This represents a useful new way of thinking about and taking into account the increased diversity of the Third World group.

The main areas of change are in market access, domestic support policies and export subsidies. On market access, NTBs are to be abolished and converted into tariffs. These and existing tariffs are to be reduced by an average of 36 per cent (24 per cent for developing countries).

Domestic support policies are to be reduced by approximately 20 per cent (13 per cent for developing countries), except where they have a minimal effect on trade distortion. These are called *Green Box* policies, and include domestic food aid and food security stocks. Developing countries which have been granted special and differential treatment may subsidize food aid distribution, investment and input subsidies.

In terms of export subsidies, the volume of exports benefiting from subsidies must be reduced by 21 per cent and the expenditure on export subsidies by 36 per cent. In addition, special provisions have been made for least developed and food-importing countries, to compensate for higher world food prices and to guard against a reduction in food aid as stocks are reduced. The provisions agreed include food aid, technical assistance, and the possibility of short-term financial assistance for normal food imports.

It is important to note that the agreement does not represent the total liberalization of agricultural trade. The cuts in support measures are only partial and gradual. Consequently the impact of the agreement is likely to be small and gradual. The anticipated increase in prices may be between 5 and 10 per cent for temperate products; for tropical products it will be less than 1 per cent (Konandreas, 1994).

The Food and Agriculture Organization (FAO) estimates that the impact on total agricultural production will be negligible (FAO, 1995). While there will be some reduction in output of temperate food products from the North, there may be a small rise in the South.

The consequent impact on trade balances will also be small. While the situation varies between different regions, in Africa the export surplus of US$1 billion in 1987–9 will be reduced to a deficit of US$1.5 million by the year 2000. (This is not all due to the Uruguay Round; population increases will also play a part.) In Latin America and the Caribbean the net result is likely to be an increase in the already positive export balance, as it will be in the Far East. In short, the agreement will adversely affect food importers, reducing the growth of consumption in the least developed and food-importing countries, while boosting the trade balance of food exporters to a lesser extent.

One of the side effects of the agreement will be the erosion of the value of preferential margins, for example those of the Lomé Convention, GSP and Caribbean Basin Initiative.[8] Many of the countries which benefit from such preferences are among the poorest of the developing countries. The potential value of the preferences from the US, the EU and Japan is expected to fall by US$0.8 billion, from US$1.9 million in 1992 (FAO, 1995).

What will change significantly is the policy-making agenda. Domestic support mechanisms, export subsidies and NTBs are all to be reduced, if not eliminated. The range of options open to policy makers has been severely restricted. However, the policies apply mainly to countries which have subsidized their agricultural sectors. They do not begin to deal with policies, common in most low-income countries, of taxing or discriminating against the agricultural sector in favour of creating an industrial sector; it can be argued that these practices have contributed to the poor performance of these sectors (Konandreas, 1994).[9]

One of the potentially significant outcomes of GATT was the creation of a new organization, the World Trade Organization (WTO), which came into effect on 1 January 1995. The question which is as yet unanswered is whether the new organization has the capacity and the political will to address questions of trade and development. Certainly many middle-income Third World states perceive their interests as being served by a more liberal multilateral system, and have given their support to the WTO. Yet China, potentially one of the biggest markets in the next millennium, has not yet been permitted to join.

Already there are realistic fears that the North will erect a new mechanism for preventing Third World exports, through high environmental and health and safety regulations (Hoekman and Kostecki, 1995). Thus while many middle-income states have accepted the logic of the free market and have an increased stake in the world trading system, the game is becoming harder to play.

The debate about the role of the state in the market is far from over. There are new approaches emerging which challenge the desirability of free trade and call for new types of protection, based on principles of equity, environmental protection and the local economy (Lang and Hines, 1993). These approaches fall under the aegis of 'another' development and ask an important question; who benefits from more free trade?

Summary

The preceding analysis leads to a number of conclusions. The volume and direction of commodity trade have changed signifi-cantly since the 1970s. In particular, trade in commodities is declining relative to that in manufactures and services. A large percentage of trade takes place within regional FTAs and bilat-eral agreements, bypassing the world market and the multilat-eral system.

Commodity trade is important for the Third World group in terms of employment and income, but in terms of volume, the EU, the USA and a number of middle-income countries from the First and Third World dominate world markets. This means that low-income countries, many of which are in Sub-Saharan Africa and South Asia, which rely disproportionately on commodity trade, can have little influence on market conditions. This places the poorest states in an extremely vulnerable position.

The Uruguay Round Agreement promised to protect the interests of the least developed and food-importing developing countries by making allowances for food aid and assistance. These are a necessary, but not a sufficient, counterbalance to the instability which has characterized commodity markets.

Furthermore, while some of these allowances are acceptable under the Uruguay Agreement, they are not acceptable within the context of SAPs.

Attempts to influence or intervene in commodity markets through ICAs or coalitions have largely failed. The success of the Cairns Group, a coalition of First and Third World states, was unprecedented. In part it can be attributed to the fact that they were large players in the market. The existence of such a coalition also demonstrates that the process of differentiation in the Third World is becoming more pronounced. As Third World countries' economic structures have grown more and more distinct, trade interests too have become increasingly so.

Part III
The Third World in the Emerging World Order

8 | The Post-Cold War World and the South

Introduction

For many years the experience of the Cold War held the world in a kind of perverse stability. The possibility of total nuclear war was sufficient to deter any major (world) wars. Not that conflict was absent; on the contrary, many smaller conflicts took place both between states (Afghanistan, Cuba, the Falkland Islands) and within states (Vietnam, Korea, Nicaragua). In all these conflicts, however, the war between the two superpowers was played out not in the First or Second Worlds, but in the Third World. Thus, although the Cold War was seemingly between the USA with its allies and the USSR, the whole world was caught in the spokes, whether or not they wished to be. Thus the claim that the Cold War dominated the international agenda between 1945 and 1989, and the way we thought about it, is no exaggeration, and the consequences for the Third World were equally significant. The end of the Cold War therefore must necessarily have had a tremendous effect on the international system and on the way we understand it.

In this chapter, the focus is on two important consequences of the end of the Cold War for the South: the changing nature of security (and implicitly of security studies, a major component of IR), and the wave of democratization now sweeping both the former Second World and the Third World, such that it is claimed we are now experiencing the *third wave* of democratic expansion.[1] We begin by looking at the post-Cold War context: the expectations and the reality of it. The next section looks at the changing nature of security, and what this means for IR and development. The third section looks at recent processes of democratization. This is followed by some case studies, which demonstrate both the fragility of the process in some areas and its longevity in others. Above all, the post-Cold War assumption of a necessary relationship between democracy and development is questioned.

The post-Cold War context

The end of the Cold War was greeted with great joy by those who supposed that it implied the end of large-scale war and the beginning of a new world order characterized by peace and stability. There was an air of triumph about politicians as they went about proclaiming the victory of the forces of good (democracy and capitalism) over evil (Communism), even before all the communist regimes had been dismantled.

The high expectations for the end of the Cold War permeated even the Third World, where the optimists assumed there would be a peace dividend. Money previously spent on arms and military arrangements would now be free to help the poor in their quest for development, reduce inequality and finance environmental protection (Bienefeld, 1994). In addition, aid would no longer be based on Cold War rivalries, but on need.

It was also assumed that, without a Cold War, the bargaining power of the Third World would increase in international forums such as the UN. Indeed, when the Non-Aligned Movement (NAM) met in 1992 it called for a strengthening of the powers of the UN, in particular of the General Assembly (Korany, 1994).

The reality of the post-Cold War world has been disappointing for those adherents of a new world order. While the era of full-scale war between the major powers appears to be over, within a year of the fall of the Berlin Wall, Iraq had invaded Kuwait. The US saw Iraq's action as 'a challenge to the new world order, in which they cast themselves as leader' (Barber and Dickson, 1995, p. 126). The international community was happy to let the US lead the onslaught and take all the credit. What was important was that the rule of law was reinstituted and that Kuwait's sovereignty remained intact. While the danger of major wars between like-minded liberal democratic states is assumed to be absent, the potential for war between smaller regional groups or civil conflicts seems to be stronger than ever (Bosnia, Rwanda, Albania, Somalia). The notion of a peaceful post-Cold War world is questionable.

The collapse of Communism in the East and the break-up of the Soviet empire have gone hand in hand with the crisis of the welfare state in the West (Hettne, 1995a). The implications for the Third World are significant. Prolonged recession has meant that politicians in the North are more concerned with domestic crises than with development problems, which seem to be never-ending. Thus 'a quietly held but pervasive view in the West is that if the Fund and the Bank can pull off miracles in the Third World, fine; if not, so be it' (Callaghy, 1993, p. 247). The post-Cold War world is a self-service one. The ever-present reality of poverty continues unnoticed unless it threatens to disrupt the peaceful world order.

In addition, along with a decrease in (politically motivated) aid because of the collapse of the USSR there are now many more contenders for a slice of the aid pie, namely Eastern European states. Furthermore, aid has not become unconditional. On the contrary, recipients are increasingly required to demonstrate that they practise good governance and do not violate the basic human rights of their population. There has always been an element of economic conditionality within the aid policies of the major economic institutions, such as the IMF and the World Bank, but the element of *political* conditionality now attached to even extant programmes is new. For example, in the latest Lomé IV Convention, which runs from 1990 to 2000, there is new emphasis on democratic consolidation and structural adjustment (Dickson, 1995).

In terms of bargaining power, it would appear that the strong are becoming stronger and the weak weaker. New hierarchies within the Third World increase the differential treatment of the international community. The NIEs of East Asia and Latin America find themselves in a more advantageous position than Sub-Saharan Africa. Africa, it seems, is no longer important to the major actors, to the TNCs, or to international banks. It produces a declining share of world output, it is severely in-debted, and, despite an increase in aid from 31 per cent of the total aid budget in 1980 to 39 per cent in 1988 (Cassen and

Associates, 1994), all other groups of Third World states performed better in the 1980s. Furthermore, Africa's room for manoeuvre, its ability to make policy choices, is severely limited by the policies of the World Bank and the IMF.

While these comments may seem very general, they are intended to give a brief overview of the reality of the post-Cold War situation for the South. Obviously some countries will benefit in some ways from the end of the Cold War, but the optimism of the early 1990s has gradually faded. The consensus which has emerged about development is couched in terms of a neo-liberal agenda which has two pillars: first, economic liberalization and the rolling back of the state to allow competitive markets to operate unencumbered (evident in SAPs), and second, the imposition of democratic regimes in the Third World, in the belief that the two go hand in hand. The new world order will be known as a prosperous capitalist and democratic international system.

Security in the post-Cold War era

What do all these changes mean for the discipline of IR and for the question of development? IR as a discipline is a product of the Cold War era; many of its theories have assumed either explicitly or implicitly the existence of a bipolar world. The end of bipolarity necessarily challenges the way in which it understands the international system and its constituent units.

Security has been a key concept in IR. It has traditionally referred to the security of the state from external armed aggression. Security, the realists argued, guarantees the very existence of the state in an anarchical international system. During the Cold War it meant the security of the state from the enemy, which for the West was Communism and its agents. The way to become secure was to amass more, or at least as much, military power as one's enemy – hence the arms race. The end of the Cold War has rendered meaningless this division of the world into two rival camps, each competing for its own sphere of influence. A conceptual vacuum has emerged: who is the enemy, and what does security involve?

The old bipolar world is no more, yet what has taken its place? The US remains a superpower but increasingly cannot take decisions without the EU or Japan. Waltz (1964) had argued that the most stable form of international system was a bipolar one, because there was no danger of an imbalance of power; all states would side with one or other power. In a multipolar world, two or more powers may side against another and create an imbalance which could lead to war. However, processes of globalization have created the perception of increased integration and interdependence between states. Consequently recourse to war is seen as less and less desirable; conflicts will be settled not by force, but by negotiation (Goldgeier and McFaul, 1992). This brings us to the recent rethinking about what security might mean in a post-Cold War world.

New security thinking asserts that security is a multifaceted process (Tickner, 1995).[2] It can no longer be seen in purely military terms (if it ever could be). Today's security threats are not as clear cut as external military threats to state sovereignty. There are many more dimensions to security; or, there are different conceptions of security.

First, it is no longer possible to focus purely on external aspects of security. In the new world order, internal threats to sovereignty have assumed new importance. It was always the case, in many Third World states, that diverse social and ethnic groups have threatened the very existence of the state (the India–Pakistan split, the Israel–Palestine question), and were often spurred on by outside interests and support. The break-up of the Soviet empire has intensified the spate of national and ethnic rivalries in Central and Eastern Europe (Yugoslavia, Chechnya). Thus security threats have arisen not so much from outside aggression 'but from the failure to integrate diverse social groups into the political process' (Tickner, 1995, p. 179).

Another way of looking at this is to point to the newness of the state in most of the Third World. Consequently, 'those aspiring to rule these countries had first and fast and in unpropitious conditions to establish a claim to political authority' (Hawthorn, 1991, p. 25). This involves the claim not only to a particular territory, but also the claim to the allegiance of the subjects of that territory and for their acceptance of being ruled. There has thus been a need to create a common identity, a national consciousness, real or imagined. If this cannot be done, if particular groups feel discriminated against or excluded from power, then the internal security of the state can become threatened by civil or military unrest (Guyana, Uganda).

Second, security has an economic aspect. It is important to have a means to generate income which can provide the basic necessities of life, including health, welfare, employment and education (Thomas, 1987) as well as secure supplies of food (see chapter 7). Indeed the World Bank has seen the achievement of food security as one of the key elements in Africa's economic recovery (World Bank, 1989). By this account, national security is about providing for the basic needs of the population. If these are not met, then it cannot be claimed that the population is secure in its livelihood. It is also more likely that social unrest will result. This in turn will threaten the internal political stability of the state.

Third, security can be seen in terms of the environment. It has always been recognized that our survival depends upon that of the planet and an ecosystem which is hospitable to human life. However, more recently (see chapter 5) we have acknowledged that human activity has the potential to threaten the ecosystem upon which we depend. In addition, it is recognized that environmentally harmful activities are not confined to any single state in either their cause or their effect. Rather the causes are diverse, and the effects can be felt throughout the world; if not now, then in the future. The global nature of environmental problems has caused academics and policy makers to rethink the questions of sovereignty – who is responsible? – and international anarchy – how can measures be enforced? Environmental degradation poses a potential threat to security (Thomas, 1992; Etkins, 1992).[3]

Most studies on the environment and IR tend towards being institutional and regime analyses (Doran, 1993, p. 55). That is, they seek to answer questions about how a competitive state system can best manage global environmental change. Thus one of the most obvious tensions which emerges in the environment in IR debate is the tension between the sovereignty of states and the global nature of the environmental problem. Indeed one of the main concerns of Hurrel and Kingsbury (1992, p. 1) is the question, 'can a fragmented and often highly conflictual political system made up of over 170 sovereign states and numerous other actors achieve the high levels of co-operation and policy co-ordination needed to manage environmental problems on a global scale?' That is, how can states and international organizations negotiate international environmental agreements which deal with the issues effectively and are widely acceptable?

The state is implicitly seen as the manager of global environmental problems. Yet the environment, because it is an issue which has implications for all people, challenges traditional definitions of sovereignty, which do not allow for global solutions to global problems except in so far as states agree to them. This approach is based on the realities of the international system, where co-operation occurs (facilitated by NGOs) when it is in the interests of states.

A wider understanding of security should not simply mean the addition of new threats to state security. It must include 'international and transnational problems which have not previously been considered part of security, but which threaten the well being and interests of states, societies and individuals as much as, or more than, military threats' (Etkins, 1992, p. 59).

The state is not the only agent of security. It is equally important for the individual to be secure. Human security is concerned not so much with weapons as with basic human dignity. The 1994 UN *Human Development Report* was focused on the question of human security, which includes safety from hunger, disease and repression (UNDP, 1994). The Commission on Global Governance (1995, p. 78) asserts that 'global security must be broadened from its traditional focus on the security of states to include the security of people and the planet.'

These different aspects of security are interdependent. The state cannot be secure unless its people are. Questions of hunger, poverty and population are important and can be addressed by a focus on the social dimension of development. Likewise the state cannot be secure unless the ecosystem is. Climate change, ozone depletion and biodiversity are issues which affect all states, yet they affect states differently. In particular, the South has been less responsible historically, but resource scarcity there may lead to conflicts. While protection against external aggression remains an important objective in a system of states, other forms of insecurity remain and need to be addressed by the international community.

The UN has been the principal international organization concerned with peace and security. It is now being called upon to do more than ensure the territorial integrity of its member states. The principle of *comprehensive security* stresses the need for cooperation, disarmament, demilitarization and transparency. The Commission on Global Governance has proposed the following norms for a comprehensive security policy:

1 That individuals need to be secure.
2 That the primary goals of a global security policy must be to prevent conflict and war and to eliminate any economic, social, environmental, political and military threats to the survival of the planet and the people and manage any crises before they escalate into armed conflict.
3 That military force is no longer a legitimate political instrument except in self defence or under UN auspices.
4 The development of military capabilities beyond that required for self defence and support of UN activity is a threat to the security of people.
5 Weapons of mass destruction are not legitimate in national defence.
6 The production and trade in arms should be controlled by the international community. (Commission on Global Governance, 1995, p. 85)

These proposals merit discussion in themselves; however, the point in this section is to highlight new and changing ways of looking at security. These ways explicitly move security away from purely military concerns and implicitly from a focus on the strongest military powers (in the First World), towards a more holistic approach which includes questions that are central to development and the Third World: human security and provision for basic needs, as well as the preservation of the environment in which we all live.

Democratization and good governance

Democracy is, like most concepts in the social sciences, essentially contestable; it defies any single or precise definition. It is nevertheless the 'buzz word' of the 1990s with respect to the Third World and Eastern Europe, not least because of the increase in the number of formally democratic states. In 1973, 25 per cent of all states were formally democratic; this rose to 45 per cent in 1990 and to 68 per cent in 1992 (Leftwich, 1993, p. 614).

There is an impression that democracy has triumphed in the

aftermath of the Cold War, and that this is unquestionably a positive trend. However, such an assumption needs further analysis. Certainly the end of the Cold War has meant that any socialist-leaning or socialist-inspired states now face an ideological crisis. The principle of the one-party state has also become discredited, although to a lesser degree. Even before the Iron Curtain fell down it was clear that economic miracles in the Soviet bloc were no more. But what does it mean to say that a state has become democratic?

A minimal, or *formal*, definition of democracy is characterized by its emphasis on regular electoral competition with full adult suffrage. This should take place within a multiparty system and involve governmental succession by constitutional and electoral procedures guaranteeing the rule of law (Qadir et al., 1993).

A wider, or more *substantive*, definition includes not only regular elections but also redistributive social and economic reforms, broadened popular participation, social justice and respect for human rights. It includes not just formal democratic structures but social democratization, so that all sectors of society participate in the benefits of democracy. It is of course arguable whether regular elections alone can sustain democracy over a long period of time. Formal democracy must be consolidated. If there are seen to be no social and economic benefits, people will soon wonder what the point of having elections is. This is particularly so where significant numbers of the population live in situations of relative poverty. The substantive definition, however, does not separate the political from the social and economic context in which it operates. It thus takes into account questions about the quality of life in all its dimensions.

Even though the trend towards formal democracy is seen as a recent one, many of the current transitions are not entirely new. On the contrary, democracy has often been tried and found wanting, and is now being tried again. For example, in many ex-British African states a period of British-inspired democracy followed political independence. However, it was later rejected as being inappropriate for the region. The constant changing of government was seen as unstable and inimical to development. It was argued that the task of economic development was so great it had to be completed before full political participation could be implemented (Rijnierse, 1993). Furthermore, democracy, where it was tried, did not necessarily bring economic development. Subsequently the failure of alternative systems of authoritarian, military or socialist rule to deliver the promised benefits led to disillusionment with the one-party state. Now these states have decided to try democracy once again, along with what is now called *good governance*. However, if one is supposed to learn from one's mistakes, it seems that unless this re-established trend delivers the goods it promises, unless it amounts to more than just a vote every five years, it too will have a short life. The next question which then comes to mind is: to what extent is the trend a permanent or a transitory one?

If democracy has proved so fragile in the past, is there a guarantee that this time around it will be more permanent? Since the 1980s many countries, starting with Latin America, have moved initially towards a period of political liberalization, 'where the fear of repression is relaxed, there are some political liberties and freedom of the press' (Rijnierse, 1993). These are minimal alterations in form, if not in substance, which give the impression of change and greater freedom. Often, as in the case of Chile in 1989, there is a move towards at least the minimal definition of democracy. Thus new political parties have emerged, and military regimes are stepping back to allow in civilian ones. In short, a much more open and competitive political culture is being established. This allows for, at the very least, the possibility of an electoral process.

According to the minimal definition of democracy, one would look for the holding of elections as a sufficient criterion. But for those who are concerned with a more substantive understanding of democracy, this would not be sufficient. Guyana for many years held regular elections, but they were internationally known as possibly the most unfair elections in the world, in which the opposition party had no chance of winning. Likewise in Central America the holding of elections has too often been fraudulently manipulated (Berntzen, 1993). In Latin America the new formal democracy has been superimposed upon immense social and economic inequalities, making its consolidation questionable. The contrast with Eastern Europe is useful, because there the revolutions forced a radical change in social relations and economic systems prior to formal democracy, which has not occurred in Latin America.

It is clear that the form democracy will take will vary from country to country. Each political, economic and social system is in some way unique, the manifestation of a particular historical process. Although democracy, if it is to have any universal value, must imply certain key ideals (for example, that power should lie with the people), there will be certain elements of the process which are culturally unique to each national entity. Thus the value of democracy may be universal, but the form will differ in different cultures (Rijnierse, 1993).

It is therefore important to look at specific processes in case studies. At the same time, there is a general trend in the Third World and in Eastern Europe, and it would be difficult to divorce these trends from each other, and from the international context. For example, in Sub-Saharan Africa, the end of the Cold War took away the ability of states to play off one power against the other, decreased the total amount of aid available, and removed the existence of a foreign scapegoat upon which to blame the failure of policy. This has made it more difficult to defend non-democratic government. The end of the Cold War initiated the process of democratization, but there were also internal processes at work, such as economic recession since the 1980s, and political repression, which led to disillusionment with authoritarian regimes. Pro-democracy movements thus emerged to challenge the legitimacy of the state.

In short, the impetus for democracy was linked to both external and internal factors. Witness the swiftness of Nigeria's suspension from the Commonwealth after the execution of pro-democracy human rights activists in 1995. All Commonwealth members, save the Gambia (which does not have a democratically elected government), voted in favour of upholding a resolution made in Harare in 1991 in support of a democratic government.

The relationship between democracy and development

There is an ambiguous and contested relationship between democracy and economic development in the South. Democratization processes have taken place in countries where economic development is low, such as in Africa, and in countries with high levels of economic development, such as South Korea, and have enjoyed a more or less continuous existence in some lower middle-income countries, such as in the anglophone Caribbean. In addition there are countries, many in the Middle East, with high levels of economic development which will certainly not become democracies in the near future. Certainly there are many more non-democratic regimes with poor developmental records, but there is no single identifiable trend.

Rueschemeyer et al. (1992) conducted a cross-national statistical survey of the relationship between capitalism and democracy. They found that while democracy is rare in agriculturally based economies, processes of industrialization transform social relations in such a way that it becomes impossible to exclude people from power. This certainly holds true for South Korea, where the impetus for democracy arose after the achievements of industrialization (Gills and Rocamora, 1992). It is also true historically in the case of Western Europe.

Industrial development in the First World was not preceded by democracy. On the contrary, democratic processes emerged after industrialization. Following on from this, the assumption of orthodox modernization theory was that democracy presupposed the existence of social and economic development. However, the countries of the North which give aid, and the international agencies such as the World Bank and the IMF, have espoused the ideology of political democracy as the logical counterpart to economic liberalism (Leftwich, 1993). Thus the World Bank, in its report *Sub-Saharan Africa: From Crisis to Sustainable Growth* (1989), implied that there was a causal relationship between political democracy and successful economic rehabilitation. Markets and democracy are seen to go hand in hand, together providing the best conditions for economic development. Indeed democracy is now seen as a precondition for development.

It is astonishing that this assumption can be made for the Third World when there is practically no empirical basis for it. The states which have been most successful in World Bank economic terms are those which have tightly managed the economy – South Korea, Singapore – without democracy. Those countries which have remained democratic throughout their post-colonial history – the ex-British Caribbean, India – are not models of economic development. If human development indices are taken into account, it is true that Costa Rica has a democratic tradition, but it is still ranked as a lower middle-income country in the World Bank tables. This two-pronged attack, linking democracy with economic liberalism, is part of a wider neo-liberal trend that has become increasingly pervasive and accepted (Leftwich, 1993), yet whose assumptions are questionable and consequences inimical to meaningful development.

The neo-liberal agenda

In the First World, neo-liberalism was a reaction to the welfare state (Hettne, 1995a, p. 112), which was accused of having destroyed the market system and thus of inhibiting full integration into the global market. 'Government had become too big, too all embracing, and too pervasive to the extent that it was now a factor in stifling initiative and dampening growth potential' (Adams, 1993, p. 146). Both Ronald Reagan and Margaret Thatcher were proponents of neo-liberalism.

In the 1980s, in response to the debt crisis, neo-liberalism became part of what has been called the counter-revolution (Toye, 1987) in development theory, mentioned in chapter 3. This argued for the abandonment of economic planning directed by the state and for a return to free markets, the principles of comparative advantage, and the development of entrepreneurial spirit; that is, for the ideal model of capitalist development. Importantly, this model has never been realized in the First World; instead it has been 'compromised by being embedded in the political and economic realities of domestic state–society relations' (Callaghy, 1993, p. 163). Thus political stability is not sacrificed for economic efficiency and vice versa. This compromise has not, however, been extended to the Third World; instead they have had to 'adjust to full orthodox liberalism without embedding it in the realities of their domestic state-society relations' (Callaghy, 1993, p. 163).

The neo-liberal agenda in the Third World is characterized by its emphasis on rolling back the all-pervasive developmental state and replacing its role in the economy with the private sector. The development of a thriving private sector and entrepreneurial spirit is seen as the basis of economic rehabilitation and growth. The World Bank and the IMF have insisted upon these changes, along with currency devaluation (designed to make exports more competitive), cuts in public expenditure and subsidies, and deregulation (removal of controls) of the economy, as a package of measures known as SAPs (see chapter 7). The successful implementation of structural adjustment is a precondition for further help from the World Bank and the IMF. It is important that states get World Bank and IMF approval as, since the debt crisis of the 1980s, other lending agencies regard this as an indicator of a safe loan.

These free market policies are not, however, politically neutral. Rolling back the state has often led to greater social and economic hardship rather than democracy, or to greater authoritarianism in an effort to stem the tide of discontent arising from such policies. Negative growth rates have meant that by 1988 per capita incomes were well below 1980 levels. Nevertheless, the World Bank continues to insist that SAPs will pay off in the long run if the policies are closely adhered to.

The literature on SAPs is large. Two main conclusions stand out, although they should be tempered by the difficulty in calculating direct correlations. While short-term reductions in BOP deficits can be achieved through contractions in the domestic economy, this is a limited achievement with many costs, which throw into question the objective of development: increasing inequality, disempowerment, political instability. Moreover, there is little evidence to date of any long-term achievements in setting the economy on a path towards more permanent growth and development (Adams, 1993). The important question which remains unanswered is to what extent the neo-liberal agenda is compatible with democracy in any but the most formal sense.

Good governance

The principle of good governance is often linked to that of democracy. In one sense it implies that democratic government is necessarily good government (hence the term 'democratic good governance'), but it is also used to refer to a more explicit exposition of the composites of good governance. Leftwich (1993) identifies three main components, or levels.

The World Bank and other international agencies place their

emphasis on administrative and managerial capacities, rather than on any explicitly political criteria. They present what they consider to be the functional and institutional prerequisites for development: 'a public service that is efficient, a judicial system that is reliable, and an administration that is accountable to its public' (World Bank, 1989, p. xii). Good governance is thus synonymous with sound development management.

This ties in with the neo-liberal thesis, put forward by the World Bank et al., that weak public sector management is responsible for unprofitable public enterprise, poor investment choices, price distortions and basically inefficient allocation of resources. Thus what is needed in Africa is 'not just less government, but better government' (World Bank, 1989, p. 5). Likewise in the 1996 *World Development Report* the World Bank argues that state intervention is justified only where markets fail, and then only to the extent that it improves upon the market (World Bank, 1996, p. 110).

The approach of governments in the North is that good governance requires not only administrative and managerial skill, but also a competitive democratic polity. This involves regular, fair and free elections, as well as respect for human rights and fundamental freedoms. Increasingly, in its explicitly political sense, democratic good governance is becoming a requirement for aid and development assistance from the First World. For example, the EU adopted a resolution on human rights, democracy and development in 1991. It states that good governance involves:

> sensible economic and social policies, democratic decision making, adequate governmental transparency, and financial accountability, creation of a market friendly environment for development, measures to combat corruption, as well as respect for the rule of law, human rights, and freedom of the press and expression. The Community and member states will support the efforts of developing countries to advance good governance and *these principles will be central in their existing or new development cooperation relationships.* (EU, 1991)

A third view is that good governance refers to not only the formal democratic decision-making structures, but also the manner in which political and economic power is distributed. In practice this means that good governance is closely allied to the idea of the minimal state and a thriving private sector. It is thus a defence of liberal values.

While it is difficult for anyone to defend bad governance, it is important to return to the question of the universality of the ideal of democracy. More often than not, what has been espoused as good governance is (Western) liberal democracy. Indeed this is the idea behind the new world order. It is highly debatable whether liberal democracy can in fact be applied to all states, in particular those which have no liberal tradition. Importantly, the value placed by liberalism on the individual and his or her rights may be anathema to societies where communities or families matter more (Parekh, 1992).

It is equally important not to assume naively that democracy is necessarily the best system of government for all states, without considering whether the right preconditions for its success exist. Democracy is essentially a matter of the distribution of power: 'democratization represents first and foremost an increase in political equality' (Rueschemeyer et al., 1992, p. 5). Thus in order to understand how or when democracy emerges, and whether it will last, the balance or distribution of power is important, not only within the state but also in relation to external interests. For example, it is clear that if there is a trend towards democracy in the Third World, it is supported by particular interests. If democracy is seen as the counterpart to globalization via economic liberalism, it is no more than 'a device by which the rich and powerful states deflect the burdens of otherwise necessary and/or painful economic adjustment onto weaker societies' (Gills, 1995).

Civil society

The idea that one of the conditions necessary for democratic consolidation is the existence of a pluralist *civil society* is gaining popularity (Leftwich, 1993; Rueschemeyer et al., 1992). 'Civil society' refers to the totality of non-governmental institutions and voluntary associations; for example, grass-roots social movements, autonomous groups and consumer watchdogs.

It is argued that autonomous groups and associations develop with increasing levels of urbanization (industrialization), which bring people together, raising both awareness and organizational capacity. Civil associations thereby strengthen the non-state classes, in particular the middle and working classes, and thus change the balance of power within society. Increasingly, the state and its agents must become accountable to the rest of society. The state becomes one (major) component and power base in society among many.

In this scenario 'capitalist development is associated with democracy because it transforms the class structure, strengthening the working and middle classes and weakening the landed upper class' (Rueschemeyer et al., 1992, p. 7) and implicitly the extent of state involvement in the economy. Thus democracy would be practically impossible in agrarian-based economies. However, although civil society may require particular social relations, which do not form in agrarian societies because communities are separated from each other, the emergence of a civil society is not automatic with industrialization. The NIEs are good examples of industrialization without democracy. The most active civil societies have emerged where more, rather than less, social and political freedom exists. Where harsh economic policies have to be effected, for example in the context of SAPs, they usually go hand in hand with the clamping down on autonomous, potentially critical groups.

While there is a link between industrialization and the growth of a civil society, it is questionable whether anything more than formal democracy can emerge where social and economic injustice remains, and this will be shown in the case studies that follow. Nevertheless, the (universal) value of substantive democracy applies even to the poor and the dispossessed.

A global civil society?

The idea of a civil society is taken one step further by the proponents of *humane governance* (Falk, 1995) and *cosmopolitan democracy* (Archibugi and Held, 1995). The end of the Cold War has made possible greater autonomy of states from the two competing power brokers, but at the same time new issues have emerged (or been recognized) which transcend national frontiers – such as the environment or the globalization of economic activity – and so limit national autonomy. While the democratic tradition assumes a national boundary in which to operate, global and regional interconnections are altering the idea of an exclusive national community. Thus the idea of the non-democratic state in isolation no longer exists (again, witness Nigeria's suspension from the Commonwealth). Such states are given the role once ascribed to the revolutionary state, 'disturbers of stability and regularity' (Armstrong, 1993, p. 299). Increasingly, states are having to answer to the international community for their internal actions.

However, many questions still remain. Who should take decisions on behalf of the international community? Can the state remain the unit of democracy, or is it important to extend the principle to the international community and its citizens? If the latter, how can this be done? 'Cosmopolitan democracy' refers to a system of global governance which is democratic at both individual and interstate levels. Importantly, state behaviour is accountable to the democratic public – the global civil society. The idea is that unless global politics becomes more democratic, it will be difficult to justify the need for democracy to states. Thus implicitly structures of decision making and power have to be altered within international organizations, such as the UN, IMF and WTO.

To date, the idea is very open-ended and loosely defined. Its exact permutations will need more working out if it is to be realized. It is nevertheless an aspiration whose appeal is heightened as global inequality increases.

Case studies: democracy in the Caribbean and Latin America

The Caribbean is unique among the Third World, having as it does a history of liberal democracies. Ten out of twelve of the anglophone Caribbean countries have consistently since independence (the earliest in 1962) held regular, free and fair elections. The exceptions are Grenada and Guyana, both of which now have democratically elected governments.

Latin America, on the other hand, has historically exhibited no such tendencies. While the type of government in the region has been extremely varied, the norm has been authoritarianism. There is at best only one long-standing democracy: Costa Rica.

However, since 1982 a new phase of democratization has begun in the region.

The purpose of this section is to look at some of the characteristics of democracy in the Caribbean and of the new democracy in Latin America. That is, we shall ask questions about the type of democracy (formal or substantive), whether it is likely to last, and whether the relationship between democracy and development is indeed a necessary one. There will be the inevitable generalizations made about these regions, which demonstrate both similarities and vast differences.

While the Caribbean history of democracy may seem short (thirty years), in fact the seeds for a democratic transition were sown in the 1930s, when, after mass uprisings, Britain began to allow more self-government which was democratic in its direction. The response to similar unrest in Central America was dictatorship. Latin America has of course been independent for a much longer period, but independence was gained not by negotiation, but by revolution.

In the Caribbean, most states are lower middle-income by World Bank standards. However, GNP per capita ranges from a low of US$530 in Guyana to a high of US$6,770 in Antigua and Barbuda (World Bank, 1996). The average is nearer to US$3,000. Despite relatively low incomes, most of the Caribbean invested in social infrastructure after independence. The Caribbean thus boasts high levels of literacy and good health care. This arguably has allowed for the consolidation of a more substantive democracy.

However, faltering growth rates and economic hardship, which eroded social policies, led to political instability in Jamaica in the 1980s. Likewise, Guyana's economic decline was accompanied by an increase in authoritarian rule. Declining domestic and international resources have led to increased insecurity from drug trafficking. With the neo-liberal agenda, the role of the state in the economy has declined. What this means is that democracy is becoming more formal than substantive. The fact that many of the poor are closely allied to a political party, and depend on that party for their survival, is one of the factors which democracy has on its side.

But democracy has not gone unchallenged. There are numerous incidences of attempted coups (Trinidad in 1990), violence which threatens to disrupt the democratic process (Jamaica in

1980), ballot rigging and intimidation of opposition (Guyana), and, in the case of Grenada, a revolution (1979) and US intervention (1983). It should not therefore be assumed that liberal democracy is a permanent fixture in the Caribbean.

Latin America's recent transition to democracy arose in part as a response to a worsening economic situation, namely the debt crisis and the failure of authoritarian governments to deal effectively with it. It is also arguable that democracy in Latin America is democracy by default (Whitehead, 1993). All other forms of government have been tried and failed. Thus what was settled for was seen as a compromise, a second-best alternative in which all the contenders for power could compete, even if it meant lowering their expectations about what could be achieved.

Implicitly this means that what has been accepted is formal democracy: regular elections and competitive politics. This trend is legitimated by the support it has received from the international community – the USA, the EU and the Catholic church. However, questions remain about whether democracy will be consolidated in all cases. Will the military be willing to take a back seat? There was a coup in Peru in 1992 led by the elected president and the military. Will harsh economic policies lead to destabilizing social unrest? There was rioting in Venezuela in the late 1980s in response to the effects of the debt crisis, followed in 1992 by two attempted coups. In many cases it is still too early to tell.

Increasingly, neo-liberal policies are being used to shape the democratic process (Whitehead, 1993). This means that the state's hold over the economy is seen as undemocratic and economically irrational. Market systems of allocation, the rolling back of the state, and privatization of the economy are being put forward as the means for social democratization (widening the distribution of power). However, it is the wealthy who thus gain or retain a stake in the economy. Furthermore, the emergence of a civil society is likely to be opposed, by illiberal and non-democratic means, should it threaten (through protests or strikes) the economic recovery of the country.

The task of becoming internationally competitive is a serious one in an increasingly globalized economy, and a difficult one with severe debts. Historically it may well conflict with social democratization. Thus it would be fair to say that democracy in Latin America is still fragile and in need of consolidation and, eventually, of being made more meaningful to the mass of the population.

In the case of both the Caribbean and Latin America, the form democracy will take depends on a myriad of factors: the international and domestic economic situation, historical factors, political culture and political institutions. There is no pattern of evolution for these factors or their effects.

Summary

The end of the Cold War has certainly changed the nature of international relations. From the point of view of the South, it has both offered opportunities, in new coalitions and trading partners, and provided new constraints, in new political and economic conditionalities. For the discipline of IR, the end of the Cold War has opened up the security agenda to new thinking, which has the potential to include concerns about development in a meaningful manner.

To argue for markets, good governance and democracy as the universally valid key to development is simplistic. The specific nature of society within which they operate needs to be taken into account. Thus any emergent trend needs to be analysed carefully: what type of democracy is emerging, and is it likely to last?

Nevertheless, democracy, even in its limited sense, offers more people a say in decision making, and helps to consolidate a civil society. Although formal democracy does not transform unequal social relations, does not eliminate poverty or misery, it can be the beginning of a process towards more substantive democracy. As such it is not to be dismissed lightly.

The neo-liberal agenda has been successfully internalized by the South. There is practically no country in the South, or Eastern Europe, which does not embrace the free market, private enterprise and trade liberalization, and the good governance ethos. Yet as we have seen in previous chapters, these policies benefit different countries differently; moreover, they may be inimical to substantive democracy.

The end of the Cold War has nevertheless led to a unified position within the North: that aid will be tied to evidence of democracy and good governance, and that the role of the state in economic development should be a minimal one. This will not necessarily ameliorate the conditions of the poorest sectors of society. The fact that so many states are now at least formally democratic is testimony not so much to the appeal of the concept as to the creation of an ideology in the North, proclaimed as universal, and exported to the South as a condition for inclusion into the new world order.

Ideas of civil society, and of a global civil society, are attempts to make the democratic process more meaningful for more people. In effect, these ideas are a recognition of the failure of many formal democracies to last, or to bring about meaningful development.

9 Development in a Global Context

The question of development

Two important questions remain: how should the question of development be defined, and who should define it? I use the phrase 'the question of development', rather than simply 'development', because I assume that development is essentially a series of open-ended questions, rather than a single, predictable end point or answer. Development cannot be reduced to a series of economic measurements. This is the important distinction between it and growth. Growth may be a necessary condition for development, but it is certainly not a sufficient one.

Hettne characterizes this as the formal–substantive dimension of the development debate. Formal approaches are those which define development in terms of 'a limited number of universally valid principles and quantifiable indicators which can be combined in a predictive model' (Hettne, 1995a, p. 254). In contrast, substantive approaches to development view it as 'historical change of a more comprehensive, qualitative and less predictable nature' (Hettne, 1995a, p. 254). The approach throughout this book has been to view development as historically produced and its manifestations as culturally specific.

It is unlikely that any single paradigm can provide a sufficient definition of what development involves. Both modernization and dependency perspectives tried to create universal laws or models, which underestimated the diversity of the Third World. Diversity is an important issue, because in recognizing it one is acknowledging not just that some economies have grown at a faster rate than others, but that there are different political, social and cultural contexts of development. It is also important in an era characterized by homogenizing influences of global processes.

Thus, in answer to the first question above, it is clear that there is no easy or satisfactory definition. Development is a contested concept. Precisely what constitutes it is both open-ended and culturally specific. In addition, as has been stated throughout, development is multifaceted. There are political, economic, environmental and cultural aspects, all of which form part of the question. Without one or other of these dimensions the development debate is narrowed down.

The question of who should define the question of development is more complex. The development debate has by and large been defined by the North and by elites in the South – the core of the core, and the core of the periphery. It has been approached with the assumption that 'the problems of the Third World could be solved by directly applying theoretical constructs derived from the study of the historical evolution of the west' (Higgott, 1983, p. 1). It has in consequence embodied assumptions about the role of the market, the value of trade, the logic of industrialization, the necessity of growth, and the superiority of Western norms and culture in the current international system.

Yet the material reality of absolute poverty and deprivation in parts of the Third World remains, and points us to the failure of the development debate, as it has been defined, to date. The perceived decline in development theory is not about a decline in the volume of literature produced; rather it stems from 'the lack of any substantive beneficial impact of this literature on the problem area to which it is addressed' (Higgott, 1983, p. 1).

It is not that there have been insufficient efforts at development. Indeed tremendous resources have been directed at the elimination of poverty and its manifestations. Furthermore, improvements in infant mortality rates, life expectancy and literacy levels have been made in most parts of the Third World. Development has become an international goal. International organizations exist for aid, debt relief, disaster relief, medical training, sustainable development and so on. It is possible to say that the principle of helping those states less fortunate than ourselves has become an international norm, although the failure of this norm to become a reality is still significant; for example, witness the paltry number of states which have consistently given the UN-recommended 0.7 per cent of GNP in aid.

The huge gap between the principle and the practice is significant (Jackson, 1990). The optimism of the 1950s and 1960s has now been replaced by a growing acceptance of the intractable nature of the problem. Parts of the world have been defined as underdeveloping, Fourth and Fifth Worlds. This points to 'the increasing identification by the international community of states that are so totally unproductive, so increasingly dependent, and devoid of any capacity for development, that they exist as no more than internationally recognised political entities' (Slater et al., 1993, p. 2); in short, to an acknowledgement that development as we know it has not taken and is not taking place.

This brings forth the need for a new debate on the question of development, one which is not so narrowly defined. Hence the need to widen the parameters of the debate from the formal, mechanical understanding to a wider, more substantive approach. The debate will also need to be one which is capable of viewing the question of development in the context of the changing global order; hence the link to IR.

The global context

At the beginning of the book I claimed that IR has been a partial discipline, excluding from its primary concerns the question of development in the international order. Development has been consigned to the realms of low (and unimportant) politics except when the international order, as it has been constructed, is threatened. This conservative disposition permeates much of IR and has meant that its view of the international order has at one and the same time been particular and exclusive.

The inclusion of development demands, at the very least, a more inclusive discipline. Or to put it another way, for IR to hold a more comprehensive view of the international order demands the inclusion of the question of development.

Two important points arise from this. The first is that development in the Third World has always been integrally related to changes in the other worlds. There is no point in the modern international system at which we can claim with any historical accuracy that a given society has developed in isolation. Thus the lack of development is not historically random, but the result of the operation of a system which all play a part in creating and transforming.

The second point is this: because of changing hierarchies in states and between states, and because of increasing (and more intense) links between states, the development question has become more complex, increasingly applicable to other parts of the world. The First World is now preoccupied with the consequences of deindustrialization, semi-permanent unemployment, social marginalization, and the movement of capital eastward. Likewise, Eastern Europe is also undergoing fundamental change and transformation, involving both integration and fragmentation, after the collapse of the Soviet empire. Questions of poverty do not only refer to absolute deprivation, but are relative to a person's expectations within a given society. The question of development is thus a shared one. Development in a global context reflects the shared experience of change and transformation and the shared context, which is the international system.

Modernization theories assumed development was about the correct internal conditions. Dependency perspectives, in an attempt to counteract this, focused on the external context. It is no longer the case – it never has been – that the external conditions alone are responsible for the lack of development, or that domestic policies alone can be blamed. The two must be taken together. Importantly, this formal distinction between the national and international, or local and global, is becoming increasingly blurred.

This is most obvious in the growing recognition that global environmental issues transcend state boundaries, and challenge traditional models of state control. It is also evident in the increasing significance of the world market for development prospects, so that even in seemingly remote parts of the world people's livelihoods can be determined by the vagaries of world market prices.

The links to world markets are not in themselves new; what is significant is the extent to which processes in one part of the world affect people in other parts through the market. For example, while cane sugar producers in the Caribbean may always have produced sugar for export, and often to protected markets, the development of artificial and low-calorie sweeteners changes the nature of the market, and consequently affects income. The rapid technological advance which has taken place (mainly in the North) means that both production processes and products can rapidly become obsolete in the global market place. This leads to the new *obsession with competitiveness* (Esteva, 1992, p. 16).

The relationship between the global and the local is not, however, deterministic. The local mediates the effects of the global, so that states respond differently to the global context. This is what Haggard (1990) has identified as a key factor in determining the relative success of export-led growth in the East Asian NIEs compared to ISI in Latin America: the different responses to the external environment. Also, some actors influence disproportionately the character of the global economy, and the manner in which we perceive it.

We have already pointed out the contested and ambiguous nature of the term 'globalization'. The increased significance of the external context for issues which previously were considered primarily of national concern is nevertheless evident. Certainly it leads to new questions about the nature of sovereignty, as the state is challenged by activities and processes at the subnational, transnational and supranational levels. It thus throws into question the possibilities of a national development strategy. In response, regional development strategies have begun to emerge in the EU, North American Free Trade Area (NAFTA), Association of Caribbean States (ACS) and Association of South East Asian Nations (ASEAN). Some academics think this is the way forward (Hettne, 1995a).

In addition, social movements at the subnational level, such as ecologism and feminism, challenge traditional approaches to development which place the state at the centre of the process. 'Another' development will be defined first at the local level, taking into account the views and aspirations of those marginalized sectors of society (Etkins, 1992). 'Alternative development is a cry for visibility, participation, and justice' (Hettne, 1995a, p. 161).

There is no doubt that globalization brings forth contradictory elements. In part it brings together regions, in part it leads to fragmentation. Not all states or regions or people will benefit equally from it. One should not underestimate the extent to which some will resist the effects of globalization. However, there are two important effects for the Third World: the globalization of principles of economic liberalization, and the pressure for formal democracy. Both of these are, importantly, part of a particular debate, characterized here as the neo-liberal agenda, and embody specific cultural values: Western liberal ones. To this extent the successful implementation and the value of this agenda to the Third World remain questionable.

Development and international relations

In chapter 1 it was pointed out that for IR to include the question of development within its ambit necessitated a more critical approach, an approach which would question not only the limited agenda of IR, but also the exclusion of the South's contribution to the international system. This goes back to the assumed universalism of theories of development and IR which originate in the North, or are based on the assumption that the South will or should mimic the North's progress, in terms of both development paths and the adoption of appropriate institutions (those reflecting the correct norms and values).

This very assumption implicitly claims that the North has been separate from the rest of the world and that there is no connection between development in the North and the 'absence of development' in the South. It also assumes that the South's contribution to the international system has been nil. This we know not to be the case. More importantly, it assumes the superiority of Western thinking about development and the international system. Hence one author claims:

> no alternative body of non western thought appears to come close to the level of sophistication exemplified by the authors considered in this book [Kant, Hegel, Rawls, Waltzer etc.]. This ought not to be surprising. The modern world has been created by Western Europeans and their offspring and thinkers in this part of the world have a headstart in understanding their creation. (C. Brown, 1992, p. 13)

Thus the best way forward can only be devised by the North because of its superior understanding of the modern international system.

This type of position has not gone unchallenged. There have been attempts to create theories based on the experience of the Third World, such as the many variants of the dependency perspective. There have also been attempts to dislodge Eurocentrism from the centre stage of social science discourse (S. Amin, 1988; W. Sachs, 1993). For IR the first task is to be aware of this bias and to seek to transcend it; that is, to adopt a self-critical approach.

It is also clear that a large body of IR literature has sought to create an objective, scientific discourse which views the world as it is, rather than as it should be. In contrast, a normative element has pervaded the development debate (even if it amounts to improvements in the standard of living for the backward societies). At one level, it is clear that all theories embody within them some normative assumptions. However, the case is being made here for a more explicit normative bias, which, in its simplest form, starts from the premise that all political action is moral action.

Thus IR must increasingly take on board questions about justice. IR does embody notions of justice, primarily that between states: interstate justice. This assumes the sovereign equality of all states. From this flow certain rights and duties, one of which is the principle of reciprocity, whereby the state recognizes the rights of others in return for recognition of its own. Yet reciprocity is not always possible among unequals. Demands for change, embodied in the NIEO, are based on the principle of redistributive justice; the redistribution of resources and power, in recognition of unequal abilities. The extension by Beitz (1979) of Rawls's (1973) *A Theory of Justice* is the best-known attempt to conceptualize how distributive justice might operate in a global context.

There are, nevertheless, many criticisms of the assumption that justice, in any meaningful sense, can be applied across state boundaries, or where there is no perceived solidarity, or no means of effecting it. Some of these objections are more valid than others. However, if we start from the assumption of moral equality of all humans within the global community – that is, that 'the interests of everyone matter, and matter equally' (Attfield and Wilkins, 1992, p. 3) – this necessarily leads to the conclusion that the current distribution of power and resources in the international system is unjust.

The value of life in any meaningful sense, as few would deny, involves particular material and non-material components: adequate food, shelter, some element of political freedom and the means to enjoy it through education, spiritual growth and so on. These may be defined as satisfying basic needs, the value of which is universal, although the form they take will necessarily be specific to the different cultural and temporal contexts in which they are effected.

Following on from this, the material reality of absolute poverty and deprivation demands action by those who are concerned with a just world order. This is not simply about 'the abandonment of our way of life, . . . but calls for the moral basis of this very way of life to be taken seriously . . . justice thus involves equality of consideration, in which basic needs are trumps, whoever's they may be' (Attfield and Wilkins, 1992, p. 5).

Importantly, if we accept that the value of basic needs is universal, but argue for the specificity of basic needs, the limitation is that we can only make minimal moral claims, such as for a minimum standard of living, or for minimal international obligations and rights. This leaves large areas of human life, and the manner in which it will be lived, open to interpretation.

The dilemma is outlined by Nussbaum and Sen. Sticking to local traditions seems:

> to promise the advantage of respect for difference: instead of telling people in different parts of the world what they ought to do and be, the choice is left to them. On the other hand, most traditions contain elements of injustice and oppression, often deeply rooted; and it is frequently hard to find a basis for criticism of these inequities without thinking about human functioning in a more critical and universal way.

On the other hand:

> the search for a universally applicable quality of human life has, on its side, the promise of a greater power to stand up for the lives of those whom tradition has oppressed and marginalised. But it faces the epistemological difficulty of grounding such an account in an adequate way, saying where the norms come from and how they can be known to be the best. It faces, too, the ethical danger of paternalism, for it is obvious that all too often such accounts

have been insensitive to much that is of worth and value in the
lives of people in other parts of the world and have served as an
excuse for not looking very deeply into these lives. (Nussbaum
and Sen, 1993, p. 4)

The third suggested component for the question of development in international relations is a political economy approach.
'A political economy approach' has become a rather fashionable
misnomer, so much so that it covers a multitude of almost
incommensurable perspectives, including liberal, nationalist,
public choice and Marxist theories. At its most basic, IPE deals
with the necessary connections between the political and the
economic in the international system, although the view of the
international system, its character and how it should operate,
and the types of question asked, differ according to the perspective.

The basic assumption that the political and the economic are
intricately related, if not inseparable, means that explanation
which gives primacy to one or the other is partial. This is more
than just a common-sense assumption. Take for example the
pervasiveness of the neo-liberal agenda, which explicitly sepa-
rates the political – the state – from the economic – the market.
Neo-liberalism undermines the welfare state in the North, and
argues for a rolling back of the state in the South. It may yet be
found that the (strong) state is the most appropriate agent for
(economic) development.

In terms of development, it is clear that the separation of the
economic from the political is not always useful. In addition,
development theory has mainly concentrated on questions about
national development strategy. In the light of previous comments, it is clear that the possibilities for national development
are both constrained and given opportunities by the international system. These relationships, between the political (often
the state) and the economic (the market), as well as the relationship between the national and the global, form the questions
which constitute a political economy approach.

What about the cultural dimension? This is one of the most
undeveloped areas in the whole debate. It is nevertheless implicit in Eurocentric assumptions about the superiority of development in the North, in the tendency towards the standardization
of culture, in theses about the end of history, and in assumptions

about what constitutes good governance. Indeed the very values and aspirations of people have been homogenized (S. Amin, 1988). If culture is a determining factor in the specificity of development, understanding cultural factors is a means towards understanding differentiation.

Differentiation

Although the question of development is shared, there is a need for recognition of differentiation between different places and times. That is, while the question is shared, its form is not the same in Sub-Saharan Africa as in Eastern Europe, or in the UK. In this book we have principally been concerned with those regions which have been marginalized from the benefits of world economic growth and/or from power, derived from a multitude of sources, in the international system, even when economic growth has taken place. The reasons for this are first that these areas have been omitted from the discourse of IR, and second that the largest concentration of unmet needs are located there. We have also been concerned to point out areas where common interests prevail within the Third World, and those where different ones do. Importantly, the issues we have dealt with are all interconnected. If we briefly look at some of the conclusions of the chapters, this interconnectedness is evident.

In terms of hunger, it is clear that a basic prerequisite for a meaningful life is that one should have access to sufficient calories, and the right mix of calories, to survive. It is also clear that the pervasiveness of hunger is linked to the manner in which agriculture has been constantly subdivided and restructured by the logic of the world market, so that what was essentially a state-based system for domestic consumption has become one which is geared towards the global market, with all its instability. Consequently, food self-sufficiency has decreased while hunger has increased, because the global market, even in its liberalized state, offers no guarantees. Hunger is therefore not a random occurrence. It is a direct result of a system of production which provides some people with access to food, while for others there is no such entitlement.

The link between the environment and development was made by the WCED (1987), and adopted and circulated at the

Rio conference (1992), but the recognition of this link has effectively been hijacked by governments which changed it to mean 'environmentally friendly growth'. There was little suggestion that the development model, which reduces development to industrial growth, had brought about the crisis in the first place.

The development and environment debate is being shaped by those international agencies (World Bank, IMF) which have championed the neo-liberal agenda. Interesting questions remain as to why this agenda, which originates in the North, has become so internalized by Southern elites. At one level, it is clear that international institutions, such as the World Bank and the IMF, espouse these policies as gospel (George and Sabelli, 1994). To the extent that a country is reliant on World Bank/IMF approval, the neo-liberal agenda may be adopted as a pragmatic response (Jamaica in the 1980s).

At another level, it is clear that the development debate was in crisis in the 1980s; neither European development theory, with its assumptions about the automatic stages of growth, nor the dependency analysis, with its limited explanatory powers, could explain the success of the NIEs and the failures in Sub-Saharan Africa. The void was thus filled by the simplistic policy prescriptions of neo-liberalism.

More significantly, the 'environmental cause' (environmental lobby groups, green political parties) has assumed its concerns can be foisted on the South, *vis-à-vis* demands for environmentally friendly timber, recycled packaging, and so on. At this extreme, the environment has become an end in itself, independent of and superior to the livelihood of people. Thus the globalization of environmental concerns is in danger of becoming one more way in which the North imposes its concerns and ideals upon the South.

The need for sustainable development remains a key issue, but it is one which is not always recognized even in the South. Most Third World states have taken on board the desire and need for industrialization and have no wish, understandably, to limit their capacity for the creation of wealth. It may well be that if the value of non-industrial goods were relatively higher, there would be little need for industrialization. This is what the EU has tried to do with its CAP, which was under severe criticism from the rest of the world in the Uruguay Round.

The irony of this quest for increased wealth is that it is not automatically translated into improvements in the quality of life. Those states which have done best in terms of the HDI, for example, have done so because they have implemented policies which are specifically geared towards the alleviation of poverty and its manifestations. This is what the welfare state had achieved in the North, but so have places as diverse as Cuba, Costa Rica, Sri Lanka, South Korea and Taiwan. Some of these states have done so without vast amounts of wealth, others with high growth rates. Some of these governments have been directly elected; in others political freedom is very circumscribed. There has been no necessary correlation between growth and development, or between formal democracy and development.

The question of development is thus a complicated one. It lends itself to no easy answers. However, if we accept that it is a question of profound significance, then it is important to keep returning to it. Recent changes in the international system throw into question assumptions about the possibility of autonomous development. Development is thus a question which impacts on all societies, though the questions and their answers will differ. In accepting this small assumption, we are moving towards recognizing the specificity of development.

Notes

Chapter 1   Development and International Relations

1 H. Williams (1992), for example, argues that IR should be understood as a theme in Political Theory and even goes as far as to argue that 'the study of political theory is the study of international relations'.

2 It is worth making a further distinction between the international, which is assumed to refer to relations between states (and nations), and the global, which encompasses non-state actors that play a role in the international system. The global can more easily take account of issues which transcend national frontiers, because it does not assume the absolute sovereignty of states.

3 These have been examined in chapters by Chan and Groom in Groom and Light (1994).

4 Idealism had little to say about the question of development, largely because it was assumed that all states save the barbaric ones operated with the same normative values. Moreover, because idealism assumed states to be the sole accountable agents, the boundaries of obligation became the political boundaries of the state. Questions of international (distributive) justice were therefore excluded from this debate (O. O'Neill, 1993).

5 National security refers to the security of the state against external aggression. It is thus defined in terms of power, that is military power, and the ability to defend one's borders successfully.

6 I have not discussed this debate because, although the behaviourists' method of analysis was significantly different from realism, the assumptions about the nature and focus of IR remained the same (Hollis and Smith, 1991).

7 A basic outline of the three paradigms can be found in McGrew (1992).

8 However, IPE as a sub-field of IR suffers from many of the ailments of IR; it tries to be a value-free social science, is heavily influenced by positivist economics, and reflects the concerns of the powerful states (Tooze, 1989). For example, it has most often been concerned with questions of the power (in the material sense) and the hegemony of states, especially of the USA.

9 IR has not historically dealt with issues of change and transformation. The study of development, in contrast, has always focused on these issues; change, after all, is what development is about. In this way it may be that development theory is better placed to understand the transitions in Eastern Europe (Korany, 1994).

10 Indeed this principle is enshrined in the UN Charter.

11 This is in effect the agent/structure debate of IPE (A. Amin et al., 1994).

Chapter 3   Theories of Development

1 Products in which a country has a comparative advantage are those which it can produce *relatively* more efficiently than other countries.

2 The diversity of the dependency perspective, as well as its origins, is covered by Palma (1978).

3 Walter Rodney is actually from Guyana. However, he was banned from the University of the West Indies campus in Jamaica in 1968, and his most influential piece of work, *How Europe Underdeveloped Africa* (1972), was written from Dar es Salaam University, Tanzania. There he became one of Africa's leading intellectuals.

4 The 'international division of labour' refers to the division of the world market between different types of production (and consumption) in different states.

Chapter 4   The East Asian NIEs

1 However, the extent of TNC involvement varies from state to state. Local firms have in fact often been given more favourable conditions, except in the case of Singapore.

2 Textiles are one of the few manufactured products which are relatively easy for Third World states to produce. However, the MFA effectively prevented Third World exports of textiles to the First World. The MFA has been much criticized and will now be phased out. The WTO is the replacement for the GATT.

3 South Korea now boasts an impressive number of unions, which have pushed the cost of labour up significantly.

4 A more detailed study of these social indicators and their significance is provided in chapter 6.

5 Where there is universal primary education, percentages may exceed 100 if some pupils are older or younger than the standard school age.

6 However, this was not the case in South Korea in 1979 (Gills, 1993).

Chapter 5   The Environment and Development

1 The hydrosphere is sometimes divided into the oceans and the cryosphere, which is composed of ice caps, glaciers, snow cover and permanently frozen ground (Legget, 1990, p. 15).

2 Malthusian beliefs are described below, p. 80.

3 It would be possible to alter this growth pattern if a shift were made towards a state of global equilibrium. This is reached when 'population and capital are essentially stable, with the forces tending to increase or decrease them in a carefully controlled balance' (Meadows et al., 1974, p. 171).

4 The South, with 74 per cent of the world population, consumes only 20 per cent of total energy (WCED, 1987). Within this there is, however, great diversity; China is responsible for 11 per cent of total Third World emissions of greenhouse gases. Likewise the NIEs are contributing increasingly to climate change.

5 For a more detailed argument about why IR has not and probably will not take the environment seriously, see S. Smith, 1994.

6 In this way it is associated with the tradition of Gaia. Gaianism seeks to explain the survival of the planet by the complementarity of life and the planet over a long period of time. This has involved a system (Gaia) which regulates and repairs itself. Importantly, the system can repair itself if it is knocked off balance, but it cannot guarantee the survival of all its parts. It is thus a very holistic belief which does not place humans at its centre.

7 A critique of the Malthusian argument on population is provided in the following chapter.

8 In particular, the question of ozone depletion has resulted in a number of protocols, or agreements between states. Indeed this success in securing agreements is often held up as a model of what the international community can achieve through co-operation in particular issue areas. For further details see Thomas, 1992.

Chapter 6   The Social Dimension

1 This (0.7 per cent GNP in aid) is the UN target agreed by the developed countries in 1970.

2 To claim we all have needs is not to claim that these needs are the same, rather that there are some similar types of need which must

be met before a worthwhile life can be lived (Belsey, 1992).

3 That is, GNP adjusted for inflation and exchange rate differentials.

4 There are many valid objections to measuring development; statistics on their own can be mechanical and devoid of humanness. Their utility lies in the fact that they downplay historical detail and make general comparisons easier. See Dasgupta, 1993.

5 The 1995 Human Development Report is specifically focused on gender disparities, arguing that women constitute 70 per cent of the world's poor people and 66 per cent of the world's illiterates, and often work longer hours than men, yet much of their work remains undervalued or unrecognized. The report thus argues that if development is meant to widen people's opportunities, it cannot continue to ignore the exclusion of women (UNDP, 1995).

6 In parts of Sub-Saharan Africa one woman dies for every fifty births. The corresponding figure for Scandinavia is one for 20,000 births (Dasgupta, 1993).

Chapter 7 International Commodity Trade and Development

1 The Green Revolution was an attempt to increase yields of certain key crops as a means to feed as many people as possible. It was particularly successful in north India. The methodology has subsequently been criticized for reducing the biodiversity of crops, and for encouraging reliance on imported fertilizers, which poorer farmers could not always afford.

2 It could for example be argued that the growth of multinational corporations (MNCs) has been primarily responsible for the multiplication of world trade. MNCs are not, however, well regulated, and certainly not by GATT.

3 In fact negotiations for the GSP took place within UNCTAD rather than GATT, again demonstrating the marginal interests of the Third World within GATT.

4 For more detailed analysis of attempts to change the nature of the international system, see Krasner, 1985.

5 The Sugar Protocol is part of the Lomé Convention, a comprehensive trade and aid agreement between the EU and sixty-nine ACP states, which was established in 1975 but whose survival is increasingly under threat (Dickson, 1995).

6 However, the importance of preferential agreements has decreased since the mid-1980s. It is likely to decrease further with the GATT measures agreed in the UruguayRound.

7 Structural adjustment policies (SAPs) require reform in three sectors: trade, finance and the public sector. They essentially aim to remove interventions, or incursions into the free operation of

market processes in all three sectors. The assumption is that economic liberalism is desirable because it is a more efficient allocator of resources and provider of incentives to achieve industrial and agricultural (economic) development. Chapter 8 discusses SAPs further.

8 The Caribbean Basin Initiative (1980) is a preferential trade arrangement for selected Caribbean states, providing access to US markets.

9 Konandreas (1994) points out some extremely interesting contradictions between the implications of the Uruguay Round Agreement for the Third World and the requirements of SAPs.

Chapter 8   The Post-Cold War World and the South

1 The 'first wave' refers to the coming of democracy to Western Europe and the USA, and the 'second wave' to the period when Latin America and many newly independent states adopted democracy. See Huntington, 1991.

2 The idea of a multifaceted, holistic security is not itself new: see for example Thomas, 1987.

3 On the other hand, Deudney (1990) argues that redefining security to include resource and environmental threats is misleading, because interstate violence has little in common with environmental problems or solutions. The methods by which security issues are dealt with, in terms of a zero-sum game, are not sympathetic to dealing with the environment.

Bibliography

Adams, S. (1993) *Worlds Apart: The North–South Divide and the International System*, London: Zed Books.

Amin, A., Gills, B., Palan, R. and Taylor, P. (1994) 'Editorial', *Review of International Political Economy*, vol. 1, no. 1.

Amin, S. (1976) *Unequal Development*, New York: Monthly Review Press.

Amin, S. (1988) *Eurocentrism*, London: Zed Books.

Anderson, K. and Blackhurst, R. (1992) *The Greening of World Trade Issues*, Hemel Hempstead: Harvester Wheatsheaf.

Anker, R. and Hines, C. (eds) (1986) *Sexual Inequalities in Urban Employment in the Third World*, London: Macmillan.

Archibugi, D. and Held, D. (eds) (1995) *Cosmopolitan Democracy: An Agenda for a New World Order*, Cambridge: Polity Press.

Armstrong, D. (1993) *Revolution and World Order*, Oxford: Oxford University Press.

Attfield, R. and Wilkins, B. (1992) *International Justice and the Third World*, London: Routledge.

Avery, P. (1993) *World Agriculture and the Gatt*, Boulder, Colo.: Lynne Rienner.

Balassa, B. (1991) *Economic Politics in the Pacific Area Developing Countries*, Basingstoke: Macmillan.

Barber, J. and Dickson, A. (1995) 'Justice and Order in International Relations: The Global Environment', in Cooper, D. and Palmer, J. (eds) *Just Environments*, London: Routledge.

Barbier, E. B. and Markandaya, A. (1989) 'The Conditions for Achieving Environmentally Sustainable Development', London Environmental Economics Centre Paper 89–101. LEEC.

Barry, N. (1981) *An Introduction to Modern Political Theory*, London: Macmillan.

Bauer, P. (1981) *Equality, the Third World and Economic Delusion*,

Cambridge, Mass: Harvard University Press.

Bauer, P. and Yamey, B. (1982) 'Foreign Aid: What is at Stake?', *Public Interest*, Summer, pp. 53–69.

Bayart, J. (1991) 'Finishing with the Idea of the Third World: The Concept of the Political Trajectory', in Manor, J. (ed.) *Rethinking Third World Politics*, Harlow: Longman.

Beckford, G. (1972) *Persistent Poverty*, New York: Oxford University Press.

Beckford, G. and Witter, M. (1982) *Small Garden, Bitter Weed: Struggle and Change in Jamaica*, London: Zed Books.

Beitz, C. (1979) *Political Theory and International Relations*, Princeton, N.J.: Princeton University Press.

Belsey, A. (1992) 'World Poverty, Justice and Equality', in Attfield, R. and Wilkins, B. (eds) *International Justice and the Third World*, London: Routledge.

Berger, M. (1994) 'The End of the Third World', *Third World Quarterly*, vol. 15, no. 2, pp. 257–75.

Berntzen, E. (1993) 'Democratic Consolidation in Central Europe: A Qualitative Comparative Approach', *Third World Quarterly*, vol. 14, no. 3, pp. 589–604.

Bhaskar, V. and Glyn, A. (eds) (1995) *The North, The South and the Environment*, London: Earthscan.

Bienefeld, M. (1994) 'The New World Order: Echoes of a New Imperialism', *Third World Quarterly*, vol. 15, no. 1, pp. 31–49.

Booth, K. and Smith, S. (eds) (1995) *International Relations Theory Today*, Cambridge: Polity Press.

Boserup, E. (1970) *Woman's Role in Economic Development*, London: George Allen and Unwin.

The Brandt Report (1980) *North–South: A Programme for Survival*, London: Pan.

Brown, C. (1992) *International Relations Theory: New Normative Approaches*, Hemel Hempstead: Harvester Wheatsheaf.

Brown, C. (1994) 'International Ethics: Fad, Fantasy or Field', *Paradigms*, vol. 8, no. 1, Summer, pp. 1–12.

Brown, K., Adger, W. and Turner, R. (1993) 'Global Environmental Change and Mechanisms for North–South Resource Transfers', *Journal of International Development*, vol. 5, no. 6, pp. 571–89.

Bull, H. (1977) *The Anarchical Society*, London: Macmillan.

Callaghy, T.M. (1993) 'Vision and Politics in the Transformation of the Global Political Economy: Lessons from the Second and Third Worlds', in Slater, R., Schultz, B. and Dorr, S. (eds) *Global Transformation and the Third World*, Boulder, Colo.: Lynne Rienner.

Caporaso, J. (ed.) (1978) *International Organisation*, vol. 32, no. 1, Winter; special issue on Dependency in the Global System.

Cardoso, F.H. and Faletto, E. (1979) *Dependency and Development in Latin America*, Berkeley, Calif.: University of California Press.

Carr, E.H. (1939) *The Twenty Years' Crisis 1919–1939*, London: Macmillan.

Cassen, R. and Associates (1994) *Does Aid Work?*, Oxford: Clarendon Press.

Cerny, P. (1994) 'Globalization and the Residual State', paper presented at the BISA conference, IPEO sub-group, University of Sussex.

Clapham, C. (1985) *Third World Politics*, London: Croom Helm.

Commission on Global Governance (1995) *Our Global Neighbourhood*, Oxford: Oxford University Press.

Corea, G. (1992) *Taming Commodity Markets: The Integrated Programme and the Common Fund in UNCTAD*, Manchester: Manchester University Press.

Cornia, G., Jolly, R. and Stewart, F. (1987) *Adjustment with a Human Face*, Oxford: Clarendon Press.

Dasgupta, P. (1993) *An Enquiry into Well-Being and Destitution*, Oxford: Oxford University Press.

David, S.R. (1992–3) 'Why the Third World Still Matters', *International Survey*, vol. 17, no. 3, pp. 127–59.

Der Derian, J. and Shapiro, M. (eds) (1988) *International/ Intertextual Relations*, Lexington, Mass.: Lexington Books.

Deudney, D. (1990) 'The Case Against Linking Environmental Degradation and National Security', *Millennium*, vol. 19, no. 3, pp. 461–76.

Dickson, A. (1995) 'The EU and its Associates', *Politics*, vol. 15, no. 3, pp. 147–52.

Dobson, A. (1990) *Green Political Thought*, London: Routledge.

Dominguez, J. (1993) 'The Caribbean Question: Why has Liberal Democracy (Surprisingly) Flourished?', in Dominguez, J., Pastor, R. and Delisle Worrell, R. (eds) *Democracy in the Caribbean*, Baltimore: Johns Hopkins University Press.

Dominguez, J., Pastor, R. and Delisle Worrell, R. (eds) (1993) *Democracy in the Caribbean*, Baltimore: Johns Hopkins University Press.

Doran, P. (1993) 'The Earth Summit (UNCED): Ecology as Spectacle', *Paradigms*, vol. 7, no. 1, Summer, pp. 55–65.

Dos Santos, T. (1970) 'The Structure of Dependency', *American Economic Review*, vol. 60, no. 21, May, pp. 231–6.

Dos Santos, T. (1973) 'The Crisis of Development Theory and the Problem of Dependence in Latin America', in Bernstein, H. (ed.) *Underdevelopment and Development*, Harmondsworth: Penguin.

Dower, N. (1994) 'The Idea of International Development: Some Ethical Issues', paper presented at the European Conference for Political Research, Madrid.

Dreze, J. and Sen, A. (1989) *Hunger and Public Action*, Oxford: Clarendon Press.

Dreze, J., Sen, A. and Hussein, A. (eds) (1995) *The Political Economy of Hunger*, Oxford: Clarendon Press.

Duden, B. (1993) 'Population', in Sachs, W. (ed.) *The Development*

Dictionary, London: Zed Books.

Dyer, H. (1993) 'Eco Cultures: Global Culture in the Age of Ecology', *Millennium*, vol. 22, no. 3, Winter, pp. 483–504.

Emmanuel, A. (1972) *Unequal Exchange*, London: New Left Books.

Esteva, G. (1992) 'Development', in Sachs, W. (ed.) *The Development Dictionary*, London: Zed Books.

Etkins, P. (1992) *A New World Order: Grassroots Movements for Global Change*, London: Routledge.

EU (1991) *Resolution of the Council and Representatives of the Member States Meeting in the Council on Human Rights, Democracy and Development*, Brussels: Bulletin of the EC 11–1991.

Falk, R. (1981) *Reflections on the World Economic Crisis*, New York: Monthly Review Press.

Falk, R. (1995) *On Humane Governance: Towards a New Global Politics*, Cambridge: Polity Press.

FAO (1994) *Uruguay Round Agreement: A Preliminary Assessment*, Rome: FAO.

FAO (1995) *Impact of the Uruguay Round on Agriculture*, Rome: FAO.

Finlayson, J. and Zacher, M. (1988) *Managing International Markets*, New York: Columbia University Press.

Frank, A.G. (1969) *Capitalism and Underdevelopment in Latin America*, New York: Monthly Review Press.

Frank, A.G. (1981) *Reflections on the World Economic Crisis*, New York: Monthly Review Press.

Frank, A.G. (1990) 'A Theoretical Introduction to 5000 Years of World Systems History', *Review*, vol. 13, no. 2, pp. 155–248.

Frost, M. (1994) 'The Role of Normative Theory in International Relations', *Millennium*, vol. 23, no. 1, Spring, pp. 109–18.

Furtado, C. (1963) *The Economic Growth of Brazil*, Berkeley, Calif.: University of California Press.

Furtado, C. (1966) *Sub deserollo y estacamiento es Americe Latine*, Buenos Aires: EUDEBA.

Gall, P. (1992) 'What Really Matters – Human Development', in Wilber, C. and Jameson, K. (eds), *The Political Economy of Development and Underdevelopment*, New York: McGraw-Hill.

Gamble, A., Payne, A., Hoogvelt, A., Dietrich, M. and Kenny, M. (1996) 'Editorial', *New Political Economy*, vol. 1, no. 1.

George, S. and Sabelli, F. (1994) *Faith and Credit: The World Bank's Secular Empire*, London: Penguin.

Gills, B. (1993) 'Korean Capitalism and Democracy', in Gills, B., Rocamora, J. and Wilson, R. (eds) *Low Intensity Democracy*, London: Pluto Press.

Gills, B. (1995) 'Whither Democracy? Globalisation and the New Hellenism', paper presented at the BISA Conference, University of Southampton.

Gills, B. and Rocamora, J. (1992) 'Low Intensity Democracy', *Third*

World Quarterly, vol. 13, no. 2, pp. 501–25.

Gills, B., Rocamora, J. and Wilson, R. (eds) (1993) *Low Intensity Democracy*, London: Pluto Press.

Gilpin, R. (1987) *The Political Economy of International Relations*, Princeton, N.J.: Princeton University Press.

Goldgeier, J. and McFaul, M. (1992) 'A Tale of Two Worlds: Core and Periphery in the Post Cold War Era', *International Organisation*, vol. 46, no. 2, pp. 467–91.

Graf, W. (1992) 'Sustainable Ideologies and Interests: Beyond Bruntland', *Third World Quarterly*, vol. 13, no. 3, pp. 553–9.

Greenfield, J. and Konandreas, P. (1995) 'The Uruguay Round Agreement on Agriculture: Food Security Implications for Developing Countries', paper presented to a meeting on the Impact of the Uruguay Round on Developing Countries and Offsetting Measures to Overcome the Negative Transitional Effects, Geneva, UNCTAD 18–19 May.

Groom, A. and Light, M. (eds) (1994) *Contemporary International Relations: A Guide to Theory*, London: Pinter.

Hadjor, K.B. (1993) *The Penguin Dictionary of Third World Terms*, London: Penguin.

Haggard, S. (1990) *Pathways from the Periphery: The Politics of Growth in the Newly Industrializing Countries*, New York: Cornell University Press.

Halliday, F. (1994) *Rethinking International Relations*, London: Macmillan.

Hamilton, C. (1987) 'Can the Rest of Asia Emulate the NICs?', *Third World Quarterly*, vol. 9, no. 4, pp. 1225–56.

Harris, N. (1986) *The End of the Third World*, Harmondsworth: Penguin.

Hawthorn, G. (1991) 'Waiting for a Text? Comparing Third World Politics', in Manor, J. (ed.) *Rethinking Third World Politics*, Harlow: Longman.

Held, D. (1993) *Prospects for Democracy*, Cambridge: Polity Press.

Hettne, B. (1993) 'Ethnicity and Development – An Elusive Relationship', *Contemporary South Asia*, vol. 7, no. 2, pp. 123–50.

Hettne, B. (1995a) *Development Theory and the Three Worlds*, Harlow: Longman.

Hettne, B. (ed.) (1995b) 'The International Political Economy of Development', *European Journal of Development Research*, vol. 7, no. 2, special issue.

Higgott, R. (1983) *Political Development Theory*, London: Croom Helm.

Higgott, R. and Cooper, A. (1990) 'Middle Power Leadership and Coalition Building: Australia, the CAIRNS Group and the Uruguay Round of Trade Negotiations', *International Organisation*, vol. 44, no. 4, pp. 591–632.

Hirst, P. and Thompson, G. (1996) *Globalization in Question*, Cambridge: Polity Press.

Hoekman, B. and Kostecki, M. (1995) *The Political Economy of the World*

Trading System: From GATT to WTO, Oxford: Oxford University Press

Hollis, M. and Smith, S. (1991) *Explaining and Understanding International Relations*, Oxford: Clarendon Press.

Hopkins, R.F. (1993) 'Developing Countries in the Uruguay Round: Bargaining under Uncertainty and Inequality', in Avery, P. (ed.) *World Agriculture and the GATT*, Boulder, Colo.: Lynne Rienner.

Huntington, S. (1991) *The Third Wave: Democratization in the Late Twentieth Century*. Norman, Okla.: University of Oklahoma Press.

Hurrel, A. and Kingsbury, B. (eds) (1992) *The International Politics of the Environment*, Oxford: Oxford University Press.

Ihonvbere, J. and Turner, T. (1993) 'Africa's Second Revolution in the 1990s', *Security Dialogue*, vol. 24, no. 3, pp. 350–2.

Independent Commission on Population and Quality of Life (1996) *Caring for the Future*, Oxford: Oxford University Press.

Ingham, B. (1993) 'The Meaning of Development: Interaction between New and Old Ideas', *World Development*, vol. 21, no. 11, pp. 1803–21.

Jackson, R.H. (1990) *Quasi States: Sovereignty, International System Relations and the Third World*, Cambridge: Cambridge University Press.

Johnson, V. and Nurick, R. (1995) 'Behind the Headlines: The Ethics of the Population, Environment Debate', *International Affairs*, vol. 71, no. 3, pp. 547–65.

Kant, I. (1991) *Political Writings*, 2nd edn, trans. Nisbet, H.B., ed. Reiss, H., Cambridge: Cambridge University Press.

Keohane, R. and Nye, J. (1977) *Power and Interdependence: World Politics in Transition*, Boston: Little, Brown.

Knippers Black, J. (1993) 'Elections and Other Trivial Pursuits: Latin America and the New World Order', *Third World Quarterly*, vol. 14, no. 3, pp. 545–54.

Konandreas, P. (1994) 'Uruguay Round Agreement on Agriculture: Implications for Developing Country Policies', paper presented at the 1994 Annual Meeting of the American Agricultural Economic Association, 7–10 August, San Diego, California.

Korany, B. (1986) 'Hierarchy within the South: In Search of Theory', in Gashar, R. (ed.) *Third World Affairs*, London: Third World Foundation for Social and Economic Studies.

Korany, B. (1994) 'End of History or its Continuation and Accentuation? The Global South and the New Transformation Literature', *Third World Quarterly*, vol. 15, no. 1, pp. 7–17.

Krasner, S. (1985) *Structural Conflict: The Third World Against Global Liberalism*, Berkeley, Calif.: University of California Press.

Lang, T. and Hines, C. (1993) *The New Protectionism: Protecting the Future against Free Trade*, London: Earthscan.

Larrain, J. (1989) *Theories of Development*, Cambridge: Polity Press.

Leftwich, A. (1993) 'Governance, Democracy and Development in the Third World', *Third World Quarterly*, vol. 14, no. 3, pp. 605–24.

Legget, J. (ed.) (1990) *Global Warming: The Greenpeace Report*, Oxford: Oxford University Press.

Leys, C. (1996) 'The Crisis in Development Theory', *New Political Economy*, vol. 1, no. 1, March, pp. 41–58.

Linklater, A. (1990) *Men and Citizens in the Theory of International Relations*, London: Macmillan.

Lipietz, A. (1995) 'Enclosing the Global Commons: Global Environmental Negotiations in a North–South Conflictual Approach', in Bhaskar, V. and Glyn, A. (eds) *The North, the South and the Environment*, London: Earthscan.

Manor, J. (1991) *Rethinking Third World Politics*, Harlow: Longman.

McGee, T.G. (1995) 'Eurocentrism and Geography', in Crush, J. (ed.) *Power of Development*, London: Routledge.

McGrew, A. (1992) *Global Politics*, Buckingham: Open University Press.

Meadows, D., Meadows, D., Randers, J. and Behrens, W. (1974) *The Limits to Growth: A Report for the Club of Rome's Project on the Predicament of Mankind*, London: Pan.

Mehmet, O. (1995) *Westernising the Third World*, London: Zed Books.

Miller, M. (1995) *The Third World in Global Environmental Politics*, Buckingham: Open University Press.

Murphy, C. and Tooze, R. (eds) (1991) *The New International Political Economy*, Boulder, Colo.: Lynne Rienner.

Nussbaum, M. and Sen, A. (eds) (1993) *The Quality of Life*, Oxford: Clarendon Press.

Ofuatey-Kodjoe, W. (1991) 'African International Political Economy: An Assessment of the Current Literature', in Murphy, C. and Tooze, R. (eds) *The New International Political Economy*, Boulder, Colo.: Lynne Rienner.

Olson, W. and Groom, A. (eds) (1991) *International Relations Then and Now*, London: HarperCollins.

O'Neill, H. (1984) 'HICs, MICs, NICs and LICs: Some Elements in the Political Economy of Graduation and Differentiation', *World Development*, vol. 12, no. 7, pp. 693–712.

O'Neill, O. (1993) 'Justice, Gender and International Boundaries', in Nussbaum, M. and Sen, A. (eds) *The Quality of Life*, Oxford: Clarendon Press.

O'Riordan, O. (1981) *Environmentalism*, London: Pion.

Palma, G. (1978) 'Dependency: A Formal Theory of Underdevelopment or a Methodology for the Analysis of Concrete Situations of Underdevelopment?', *World Development*, vol. 6, no. 7/8, pp. 881–924.

The Palme Report (1982) *Common Security: A Programme for Disarmament*, London: Pan.

Pantin, D. (1994) *The Economies of Sustainable Development in Small Caribbean Islands*, Jamaica and Trinidad: University of the West Indies, Centre for Environment and Development, Jamaica, and

Department of Economics, Trinidad.

Parekh, B. (1992) 'The Cultural Particularity of Liberal Democracy', in Held, D. (ed.) *Prospects for Democracy*, Cambridge: Polity Press.

Paterson, M. (1994) 'The Politics of Climate Change after Rio', in Thomas, C. (ed.) *Rio: Unravelling the Consequences*, Ilford: Frank Cass.

Pepper, D. (1993) *Eco Socialism*, London: Routledge.

Platteau, J. (1991) 'Traditional Systems of Social Security and Hunger Insurance', in Ahmad, E. (ed.) *Social Security in Developing Countries*, Oxford: Clarendon Press.

Prebisch, R. (1950) *The Economic Development of Latin America and its Principal Problems*. New York: United Nations.

Qadir, S., Clapham, C. and Gills, B. (1993) 'Democratisation in the Third World', *Third World Quarterly*, vol. 14, no. 3, special issue.

Rahnema, M. (1993) 'Poverty', in Sachs, W. (ed.) *The Development Dictionary*, London: Zed Books.

Rawls, J. (1973) *A Theory of Justice*, Oxford: Oxford University Press.

Redclift, M. (1987) *Sustainable Development*, London: Methuen.

Reynolds, C. (1973) *Theory and Explanation in International Politics*, London: Martin Robertson.

Richardson, D. (1994) 'Sustainable Development: Terminological Implications of Politics and Political Implications of Terminology', paper presented at the BISA Conference, University of York.

Riddell, R. (1981) *Ecodevelopment*, Aldershot: Gower.

Rijnierse, E. (1993) 'Democracy in Sub-Saharan Africa? Literature Overview', *Third World Quarterly*, vol. 14, no. 3, pp. 647–64.

Ritson, C. and Harvey, D. (eds) (1996) *The CAP and the World Economy*, Oxford: CAB International.

Rodney, W. (1972) *How Europe Underdeveloped Africa*, London: Bogle L'Ouverture.

Rostow, W. W. (1960) *The Stages of Economic Growth*, Cambridge: Cambridge University Press.

Rowlands, I. (1993) 'Paying for Sustainable Development', *Oxford International Review*, vol. v, no. 1, Winter, pp. 28–31.

Roxborough, I. (1979) *Theories of Underdevelopment*, London: Macmillan.

Rueschemeyer, D., Stephens, E.H. and Stephens, J. (1992) *Capitalist Development and Democracy*, Cambridge: Polity Press.

Ruggie, J.G. (1983) 'International Regimes, Transactions and Change: Embedded Liberalism in the Post War Economic Order', in Krasner, S. (ed.) *International Regimes*, Ithaca, N.Y., and London: Cornell University Press.

Sachs, I. (1974) 'Eco Development', *Ceres*, vol. 17, no. 4, pp. 17–21.

Sachs, W. (ed.) (1992) *The Development Dictionary*, London: Zed Books.

Sachs, W. (ed.) (1993) *Global Ecology*, London: Zed Books.

Saurin, J. (1994) 'Global Environmental Degradation, Modernity, and Environment Knowledge', in Thomas, C. (ed.) *Rio: Unravelling the Consequences*, Ilford: Frank Cass.

Scott, J. (1995) *Development Dilemmas in the EC*, Buckingham: Open University Press.

Seabright, P. (1993) 'Pluralism and the Standard of Living', in Nussbaum, M. and Sen, A. (eds) *The Quality of Life*, Oxford: Clarendon Press.

Sen, A. (1981) *Poverty and Famines: An Essay on Entitlement and Deprivation*, Oxford: Clarendon Press.

Sen, A. (1992) 'Development: Which Way Now?', in Wilber, C. and Jameson, K. (eds) *The Political Economy of Development and Underdevelopment*, New York: McGraw-Hill.

Sen, A. (1993) 'Capability and Well Being', in Nussbaum, M. and Sen, A. (eds) *The Quality of Life*, Oxford: Oxford University Press.

Sen, P. (1995) 'Environmental Policies and North–South Trade: A Selected Survey of the Issues', in Bhaskar, V. and Glyn, A. (eds) *The North, the South and the Environment*, London: Earthscan.

Shaw, M. (1994) *Global Society and International Relations*, Cambridge: Polity Press.

Shue, H. (1992) 'The Unavoidability of Justice', in Hurrel, A. and Kingsbury, B. (eds) *The International Politics of the Environment*, Oxford: Oxford University Press.

Skogstad, G. (1994) 'Agricultural Trade and the International Political Economy', in Stubbs, R. and Underhill, G. (eds) *Political Economy and the Changing Global Order*, Basingstoke: Macmillan.

Slater, R., Schutz, B. and Dorr, S. (1993) *Global Transformation and the Third World*, Boulder, Colo.: Lynne Rienner.

Smith, M. (1992) 'Modernization, Globalization and the Nation State', in McGrew, A. and Lewis, P. (eds) *Global Politics*, Cambridge: Polity Press.

Smith, S. (1994) 'The Environment on the Periphery of International Relations', in Thomas, C. (ed.) *Rio: Unravelling the Consequences*, Ilford: Frank Cass.

Smith, S. (1995) 'The Self Images of a Discipline' in Booth, K. and Smith, S. (eds) *International Relations Theory Today*, Cambridge: Polity Press.

Spraos, J. (1980) 'The Statistical Debate on Net Barter Terms of Trade between Primary Commodities and Manufactures', *Economic Journal*, vol. 90, pp. 107–28.

Standing, G. (1992) 'Global Feminization through Flexible Labour', in Wilber, C. and Jameson, K. (eds) *The Political Economy of Development and Underdevelopment*, New York: McGraw-Hill.

Strange, S. (1988) *States and Markets*, London: Pinter.

Sunkel, O. (1969) 'National Development Policy and External Dependency in Latin America', *Journal of Development Studies*, vol. 6, no. 1, pp. 23–48.

Sunkel, O. (1971) 'Social Change and Frustration in Chile', in Godoy, H. (ed.) *Structura Social de Chile*, Santiago: Editorial Universitaria.

Tan, G. (1993) 'The Next NICs of Asia', *Third World Quarterly*, vol. 14, no. 1, pp. 57–73.

Thacher, P. (1992) 'The Role of the UN', in Hurrel, A. and Kingsbury, B. (eds) *The International Politics of the Environment*, Oxford: Oxford University Press.

Thomas, C. (1987) *In Search of Security: The Third World in International Relations*, Hemel Hempstead: Harvester Wheatsheaf.

Thomas, C. (1992) *The Environment in International Relations*, London: RIIA/Chameleon Press.

Thomas, C. (ed.) (1994) *Rio: Unravelling the Consequences*, Ilford: Frank Cass.

Tickner, J. A. (1995) 'Revisioning Security', in Booth, K. and Smith, S. (eds) *International Relations Theory Today*, Cambridge: Polity Press.

Tooze, R. (1989) 'International Political Economy and International Relations: From Enfant Terrible to Child Prodigy', in Dyer, H. and Mangasarian, L. (eds) *The Study of International Relations*, Basingstoke: Macmillan.

Toye, J. (1987) *Dilemmas of Development: Reflections on the Counter Revolution in Development Theory and Policy*, Oxford: Blackwell.

Tussie, D. (1987) *The Less Developed Countries and the World Trade System: A Challenge to the GATT*, London: Pinter.

Tussie, D. (1993) 'Holding the Balance: The Cairns Group in the Uruguay Round', in Tussie, D. and Glover D. *The Developing Countries in World Trade: Policies and Bargaining Strategies*, Boulder, Colo. Lynne Rienner.

Tussie, D. and Agosin, M. (eds) (1993) *Trade and Growth: New Dilemmas in Trade Policy*, London: Macmillan.

Tussie, D. and Glover, D. (1993) *The Developing Countries in World Trade: Policies and Bargaining Strategies*, Boulder, Colo.: Lynne Rienner.

Underhill, G. (1994) 'Conceptualising the Changing Global Order', in Stubbs, R. and Underhill, G. (eds) *Political Economy and the Changing Global Order*, London: Macmillan.

UNDP (1992) *Human Development Report*, New York: Oxford University Press.

UNDP (1994) *Human Development Report*, New York: Oxford University Press.

UNDP (1995) *Human Development Report*, New York: Oxford University Press.

Valenzuela, J. and Valenzuela, A. (1981) 'Modernization and Dependency: Alternative Perspectives in the Study of Latin American Underdevelopment', in Munoz, H. (ed.) *From Dependency to Development*, Boulder, Colo.: Westview Press.

Wallerstein, I. (1974) *The Modern World System*, New York: Academic Press.

Wallerstein, I. (1979) *The Capitalist World Economy*, New York: Cambridge University Press.

Waltz, K.N. (1964) 'The Stability of a Bipolar World', *Daedulus*, no. 93, pp. 881–909.

WCED (1987) *Our Common Future* (the Bruntland Report), Oxford: Oxford University Press.

Whitehead, L. (1993) 'The Alternatives to Liberal Democracy: A Latin American Perspective', in Held, D. (ed.) *Prospects for Democracy*, Cambridge: Polity Press.

Wilber, C. and Jameson, K. (eds) (1992) *The Political Economy of Development and Underdevelopment*, New York: McGraw-Hill.

Williams, H. (1992) *International Relations in Political Theory*, Buckingham: Open University Press.

Williams, M. (1993) 'Re-articulating the Third World Coalition: The Role of the Environmental Agenda', *Third World Quarterly*, vol. 14, no. 1, pp. 7–29.

Williams, M. (1994) *International Economic Organisations and the Third World*, Hemel Hempstead: Harvester Wheatsheaf.

World Bank (1981) *Accelerated Development in Sub-Saharan Africa: Agenda for Action* (the Berg Report), Washington, D.C.: World Bank.

World Bank (1986) *World Development Report*, Oxford: Oxford University Press.

World Bank (1989) *Sub-Saharan Africa: From Crisis to Sustainable Growth*, Washington, D.C.: World Bank.

World Bank (1994) *World Development Report*, Oxford: Oxford University Press.

World Bank (1996) *World Development Report*, Oxford: Oxford University Press.

Index